THE BIRTH OF
MODERN AMERICA
1820–1850

THE BIRTH OF

MODERN AMERICA

AMERICA

1820–1850

BY DOUGLAS T. MILLER

PEGASUS   NEW YORK

To Elwell

CONTENTS

ILLUSTRATIONS

PREFACE

HENRY ADAMS, WHO WAS BORN IN 1838, LOOKED BACK upon the early years of his childhood as an historic turning point more significant than "had ever happened before in human experience." For him "the old universe was thrown into the ash heap and a new one created. He [Henry Adams] and his eighteenth-century . . . Boston were suddenly cut apart—separated forever—in act if not in sentiment, by the opening of the Boston and Albany Railroad; the appearance of the first Cunard steamers in the bay; and the telegraphic messages which carried from Baltimore to Washington the news that Henry Clay and James K. Polk were nominated for the Presidency. This was May, 1844; he was six years old; his new world was ready for use, and only fragments of the old met his eyes." To Adams these three events in 1844 symbolized the arrival of modern America—an America of power and speed, a mechanized, fragmented world from which he himself felt always alienated.

Historians, concerned less with personal and symbolic experience than the reminiscing Adams, realize, of course,

that the past does not divide itself neatly from one age to
the next. History is a constant process of change—every
age being both transitional and formative.

Nevertheless, while it would be questionable to date the
genesis of modern times in a particular month of 1844,
there is much truth in Adams' assessment. If one takes
not a precise date but the broad period from the 1820's
through the 1840's, an impressive list could be compiled
of such events as the opening of new railways, the arrival
of transatlantic steamers, or the transmission of telegraphic messages that were indicative of a new and innovative era. The fact that the three things picked by
Adams to symbolize the new age all involved advanced
technology is also significant. Certainly the most obvious
factor differentiating this age from previous periods was
the application of technology to transportation, communication, and industry. Further, Adams' statement that
by 1844 "only fragments" of the old order remained also
bears up well under historical investigation. Most of the
basic changes which set modern America off from its
premodern past were clearly apparent to astute observers
of the 1820's and 1830's. Between the first decades of
the nineteenth century and the years of Andrew Jackson's presidency, America changed from a traditional, pre-
industrial society that was slow to accept innovations,
to a modern capitalistic state in which people believed
that society could be transformed. The mid-1840's, therefore, were well within the modern era.

The revolutions in industry and transportation spawned
by applied technology were not the only aspects of American modernization. Equally significant were the moral,
psychological, ideological, and political changes in the
period from the 1820's through the 1840's. It was a complex combination of changes that made this a modern age.

Innovations took many forms. For the first time the rate

of sustained urban growth exceeded that of the population as a whole. The percentage or persons engaged in non-agricultural employment also sharply increased. From the earliest colonial settlement up until about 1815, persons involved in commerce, industry, administration, and the professions had made up roughly fifteen per cent of the population; by 1840, however, over thirty-six per cent of Americans were so employed. It was also during these years that a notable rise in per capita income began as industrialism became self-sustaining, and national markets for mass-produced products developed. Rapid geographical expansion and agricultural specialization accompanied these changes.

The extent of industrial and geographical growth during the first half of the nineteenth century helped give rise to a new faith in progress. All manner of human ills, it was believed, could be overcome. A variety of would-be religious and secular utopias were conceived and established. Other persons, less visionary perhaps than the utopians, though still perfectionists, organized to rid the world of war, slavery, intemperance, and other evils. Most individuals, whether participating reformers or not, shared the faith in human betterment and believed that perfection itself could be achieved in the foreseeable future.

Yet, if the innovations of the twenties through the forties gave rise to high hopes, they also created conflicts and tensions. During these years institutions and values, inherited from Europe and adapted to the American environment through the two hundred years of the colonial and early national periods, were forced to adjust to rapidly altering conditions. In many cases accustomed organizations, beliefs, and practices proved inadequate and broke down or were sharply modified. The family, for instance, traditionally a large kinship unit, of necessity became more nuclear as younger persons sought opportunities in the rising cities or on the expanding frontier. Similarly, new economic opportunities for women in industry tended to modify the traditional male and female roles. Personal relationships generally became less stable and less communal. The very belief that one's inherited economic and social status *could* be changed gave rise to the notion that it *should* be changed. Yet there existed no secure sense of what one should achieve. The result was a confusion of values and goals. Insecurity and anxiety became hallmarks of the American character in this period and have remained so to this day.

Many persons suffered not only from psychological dislocation, but from economic exploitation as well. For thousands of workers—women, children, and immigrants particularly—the great economic growth of the era meant only increased regimentation of their labor at wages that seldom reached beyond the barest subsistence.

It would be pleasant to relate that the various crises and tensions created by modernization were suddenly resolved by the triumphant appearance on the political scene of Andrew Jackson—uniting West with East, spreading democracy everywhere. Such, however, was not the case. Two-party politics as it re-emerged in the Jacksonian era was characterized by coalition parties seeking to win the support of the broadest possible electorate. These parties tended to be conservative and nonideological. Basic economic, social, and moral issues were either ignored or compromised; they were seldom dealt with in an effective manner.

To concentrate on politics then, as most historians have done, is misleading for two basic reasons: first, because the major social, economic, psychological, and intellectual innovations of the period were only indirectly related to the political battles and policies of Whigs and Democrats;

second, because an exclusive examination of politics gives a false picture of consensus. Recent scholarship has shown that the ideological gulf between the two parties was not so great as was once believed and that both parties appealed to similar middle-class constituencies. Furthermore, it is generally agreed today that both parties operated within a liberal democratic framework that accepted constitutional government and majority rule. While this is true, if it is accepted as a reflection of the harmonious, middle-class, capitalistic nature of American society, it gives a false picture. Conflict was rampant in the era, running the gamut from subtle psychological tensions caused by the clash between traditional and modern values, to out-and-out mob violence. Such disputes, however, were seldom expressed in the period's politics. Consequently, by centering on politics, the complex conflicts in the country are reduced to relatively unimportant squabbles over such issues as the tariff, spoils, the Bank, land and Indian policy, and the affairs of Peggy Eaton.

Many contemporaries were aware of the nonessential nature of national politics. Today we assume that presidential elections are of major significance, but in the days of Jackson, when the federal government was small and distant, this was not the case. The only national election of that period to attract a sizable portion of the eligible electorate (about seventy-eight per cent) was the Log Cabin campaign of 1840 in which every conceivable electioneering device was used to bring out the vote. Many of the most heated and significant battles of the time took place on the state and local political level or outside of politics altogether.

Of the innumerable middle- and upper-class Europeans who came to view and report on American life in the second quarter of the nineteenth century, almost none treated the evolution of American society in terms of political history. This was not because these writers were disinterested in politics—most were politically conscious and curious about political democracy in the United States. Rather, it stemmed from their sensing that the role of political parties and the actions of the government in Washington were incidental to such fascinating and important phenomena as American manners, morals, religion, commerce, industry, and internal improvements. The chapter titles of the most analytical and important books by foreign observers such as Alexis de Tocqueville, Michel Chevalier, Harriet Martineau, and Francis Grund read like recent works in cultural anthropology or sociology, with chapters on public opinion, the family, class structure, land-tenure, and social values.

The written perceptions of European travelers vary greatly in their present-day worth; even the best of these studies tend toward superficiality, overgeneralization, and bias. But what the student of Jacksonian America would do well to appropriate is the general conceptual framework that most European writers used in analyzing this country. More can be learned of the complexities of American society by conceiving it as a totality with sociological, psychological, intellectual, and economic dimensions in addition to its political realities.

There are many reasons, of course, why American historians have repeatedly focused on the politics of this period. One obvious explanation is that history has been traditionally conceived as the record of past politics. Then too there is the commanding figure of Jackson, whose willful and dramatic career fascinated his contemporaries and later Americans alike. To historians this became "the age of Jackson." In a broader sense this concentration on Jackson and his policies represented the still common textbook tendency to organize periods of American history around presidential administrations.

But the major reason that the political victory of the Jacksonians has seemed so significant is that until recently it has been viewed as the triumph of democracy. From the time of Turner and Beard to the publication of Arthur M. Schlesinger, Jr.'s *Age of Jackson* in 1945, it was assumed that Jackson's election signified the successful emergence of the common man in American politics. As long as this was believed, it was natural that historians would emphasize the importance of Jacksonian politics.

Recent scholarship, however, has challenged the traditional interpretations. For one thing, the idea of a sudden flowering of democracy in the late 1820's and 1830's has been sharply criticized. A number of writers have attacked the progressive dichotomy which saw history as a recurring struggle between conservative and democratic forces. America, such authors maintain, has always been basically a middle-class, democratic society; the common man has never been submerged and therefore he did not dramatically re-emerge as a Jacksonian Democrat in 1828. Other historians have shown specifically that most of the democratic innovations, such as the extension of the suffrage, preceded the triumph of the Jacksonians and were unrelated to that movement. Finally, several recent studies have intimated that the egalitarian aspects of the age have been overemphasized, and that the political, social, and economic equality was more rhetorical than real. In fact not only has the dominance of the common man been challenged, but also it has been claimed that the economic development of the time helped create sharper social stratification.

These new interpretations suggest the need to de-emphasize politics and to re-evaluate the major themes of the era. This does not mean, however, that the Middle Period is less significant than was once believed. On the contrary, I would propose that it is more so. By breaking from the previous focus on politics and democracy and treating the era in relation to its social, economic, intellectual, and psychological realities, the importance of these years as a major age of innovation becomes apparent. During the decades from the 1820's through the 1840's modern America was born, and its birth profoundly altered the subsequent course of American history. It is hoped that this book will help to shift future historical emphasis toward such a broader perspective.

Thanks are due to Professors William B. Hixson, Jr., Peter D. Levine, Gilman M. Ostrander, Norman Pollack, and James H. Soltow for their perceptive readings of the entire manuscript. I am also grateful to my graduate students Dale M. Herder, Blaine E. McKinley, Lawrence E. Mintz, and Mara Wolfgang, who served as a critical sounding board during early stages of this study and who read the completed manuscript.

A summer stipend from the National Endowment for the Humanities in 1968, followed by a research term off provided by Michigan State University gave me six uninterrupted months during which most of this book was written. An All-University Grant from Michigan State helped defray typing and other expenses.

Unlike some scholars' wives, Sheila has not been my editorial girl-Friday. She is loving and a pleasure to live with and that to me is the best collaboration.

And, finally, I would like this book to serve as a small tribute to my late father.

THE BIRTH OF MODERN AMERICA

1820–1850

CHAPTER ONE

"Everything's Changed"

In 1829, THE YEAR ANDREW JACKSON TOOK OFFICE AS the seventh President of the United States, John Quidor, an eccentric but brilliant artist, exhibited a painting entitled *The Return of Rip Van Winkle* (plate 1). Based on Washington Irving's popular story, Quidor's painting shows a grotesque, large, bearded, old man trying to orient himself in an unfamiliar world. He appears alienated and hostile as he gazes anxiously at the strange crowd and looks for a familiar face. Around him mills the town's coarse, curious, frenzied, beardless population. Although in Irving's story Rip had fallen asleep in the period before the Revolution and awoke presumably in the 1790's, his awaking from a twenty-year sleep to discover an alien world was a better anecdote for the period in which Irving published the story, 1819; by the time Quidor illustrated Rip's return the tale had become, if anything, even more representative.[1]

Change appeared everywhere in the years following the War of 1812, and Irving and Quidor capture this in their

---

[1] The popularity of Irving's story increased in the Jacksonian era. In 1829 a play by John Kerr, based on Rip Van Winkle, opened in Washington and for the next generation was standard American theater fare.

characterizations of Rip Van Winkle. To the returning old man the transformation of society was more than that wrought by mere time. "The very character of the people seemed changed," he observed. "There was a busy, bustling, disputatious tone about it, instead of the accustomed phlegm and drowsy tranquility . . . everything's changed." The town had grown larger and more populous. "There were rows of houses which he had never seen before, and those which had been familiar haunts had disappeared. Strange names were over the doors—strange faces at the windows—everything was strange."

Many contemporaries were aware that American society was being rapidly altered in the generation after the War

1.　John Quidor, *The Return of Rip Van Winkle*

Courtesy of the National Gallery of Art, Washington, D.C. Andrew Mellon Collection, 1942.

of 1812. "We stand this moment," stated Chancellor James Kent at New York's 1821 Constitutional Convention, "on the brink of fate, on the very edge of the precipice . . . . We are no longer to remain plain and simple republics of farmers, like New-England colonists, or the Dutch settlements on the Hudson. We are fast becoming a great nation, with great commerce, manufactures, population, wealth, luxuries, and with the vices and miseries that they engender." Three years later Daniel Webster proclaimed: "Our age is wholly of a different character, and its legislation takes another turn. Society is full of excitement . . . ." "The present," stated another American in the late 1820's, "is distinguished from every preceding age by a universal ardour of enterprise in arts and manufactures."

It would be impossible to date precisely when America changed from a tenacious, traditional society, fearful of innovation and not given to seeking riches by speculative shortcuts, to a shifting, restless, and insecure world bent on finding quicker ways to wealth than the plodding path of natural increase. But that such a shift did take place in the years between the War of 1812 and the time of Jackson is clearly evident. As Henry Cabot Lodge, who was born in 1850, noted in his *Early Memories:* "there was a wider difference between the men who fought at Waterloo and those who fought at Gettysburg or Sedan or Mukden than there was between the followers of Leonidas and the soldiers of Napoleon." To Lodge "the application of steam and electricity to transportation and communication made a greater change in human environment than had occurred since the earliest period of recorded history." In his estimate "the break between the old and the new" was completed by the 1830's.

Lodge's friend, Henry Adams, who also believed that the advent of such things as steamships, railroads, and the telegraph had thrown "the old universe . . . into the ash-heap," had, as an historian, described that old universe in some detail. His voluminous history of the administrations of Jefferson and Madison remains a landmark of American historical writing. Of the many chapters in this study the most memorable are the first six, in which Adams painted a panoramic picture of society and thought in the United States around the year 1800. This pioneering effort in social and intellectual history still constitutes one of the most brilliant surveys of any period of American history.

The republic that Adams depicted in 1800 seems remote to the historian immersed in the study of Jackson's America. It was a society in which, as Adams wrote, "experience forced on men's minds the conviction that what had ever been must ever be. At the end of the eighteenth century nothing had occurred which warranted the belief that even the material difficulties of America could be removed." The result of this was, Adams claimed, "that the popular character was likely to be conservative . . . . Great as were the obstacles in the path of the United States, the greatest obstacle of all was in the human mind. Down to the close of the eighteenth century no change had occurred in the world which warranted practical men in assuming that great changes were to come."

Most Americans were farmers, and although farming could give a man modest comfort, or at least security, it provided little more. "The Saxon farmer of the eighth century," wrote Adams, "enjoyed most of the comforts known to Saxon farmers of the eighteenth . . . . America was backward. Fifty or a hundred miles inland more than half the houses were log-cabins, which might or might not enjoy the luxury of a glass window." Cash crops, except near large towns or on waterways, were rare. A recent quantitative study of *The Social Structure of Revolutionary America* by Jackson Turner Main estimates that "the great majority of farms produced only a small cash surplus . . . ."

Professor Main considered a four per cent annual return
on the value of one's property to be high. Except for a few
gentlemen farmers and some innovating yeomen who experimented with such scientific innovations as crop rotation
and fertilization, farming methods were primitive and
wasteful. Yields were low, and hand labor predominated.
In 1806, Richard Parkinson, a disgruntled Englishman who
had tried farming in America, warned any of his countrymen who might be thinking of migrating to the United
States that they "will have to chop up trees, and cultivate
the land by the hoe and pick-axe, instead of the plough and
harrows." Plows, of course, did exist, but most were of
wood, sometimes plated with tin. Plowing an acre with a
team of oxen was a good day's work. Labor-saving machines
were few, while livestock, according to a foreign visitor, was
"lean and rangy."

But the main factor that limited the economic opportunity of the farmer was poor transportation. At the beginning of the nineteenth century the conditions of travel in
America had advanced little beyond the primitive. Where
navigable waterways were not available, crude roads and
trails made their way. Not until the Philadelphia to Lancaster turnpike opened in 1794—some sixty-two miles of
stone and gravel pavement—did the United States have
anything that could be called an improved road. The trans-
Appalachian region was virtually cut off from the Atlantic
seaboard. As Adams wrote: "The valley of the Ohio had
no more to do with that of the Hudson, the Susquehanna,
the Potomac, the Roanoke, and the Santee, than the valley
of the Danube with that of the Rhone, the Po, or the
Elbe . . . . The idea of bringing the Mississippi River, either
by land or water, into close contact with New England,
must have seemed wild."

The ability of the entire economy to grow was severely
limited by this lack of adequate transportation. Markets

were at best local and profits small; consequently the farmer had little incentive to produce more goods. As late as 1810 Congressman Peter B. Porter from western New York testified that "the single circumstance of want of a market is already beginning to produce the most disastrous effect, not only on the industry, but on the morals of the inhabitants. Such is the fertility of their land that one-half their time spent in labor is sufficient to produce every article their farms are capable of yielding, in sufficient quantities for their own consumption, and there is nothing to incite them to produce more. They are, therefore, naturally led to spend the other part of their time in idleness and dissipation."

Adams reached similar conclusions in regard to the indolence of the average American in the early nineteenth century. "Idling," he wrote, "seemed to be considered a popular vice, and was commonly associated with tippling. So completely did the practice disappear in the course of another generation that it could scarcely be recalled as offensive; but in truth less work was done by the average man in 1800 than in aftertimes, for there was actually less work to do . . . . The roar of the steam-engine had never been heard in the land, and the carrier's wagon was three weeks between Philadelphia and Pittsburgh. What need for haste when days counted for so little? Why not lounge about the tavern when life had no better amusement to offer? Why mind one's own business when one's business would take care of itself?"

In the Atlantic port cities, of course, economic opportunity was greater. The French Wars provided unprecedented chances for the commercial classes. Exports, re-exports, and imports swelled, increasing the country's prosperity, and helping to generate the new idea that great wealth was a possibility. In the course of an eighteen-month period during 1806–07, the Baltimore trading firm of Robert Oliver,

one of America's first millionaires, netted a profit of
$775,000. Yet even the merchants led a more leisurely life
than did their counterparts a generation later. As Adams
wrote of the early nineteenth-century Boston shippers: "a
mail thrice a week to New York, and an occasional arrival
from Europe or the departure of a ship to China, left ample
leisure for correspondence and even gossip."

Manufacturing was in its infancy. The elaborate plans
of Alexander Hamilton and Tench Coxe to secure govern-
mental support for industry had come to naught. Hamilton's own heavily financed cotton-spinning mill located
along the falls of the Passaic River at Paterson, New Jersey,
failed within a few years of its inception. And while Samuel
Slater's efforts had been successful in establishing the cotton textile industry, by 1800 there were only seven small
Arkwright mills operating in the entire country.

Americans were slow to back innovations. As late as 1803,
Benjamin Latrobe, America's foremost engineer and archi-
tect, reported only five steam engines in use in the United
States—one pumping water for Aaron Burr's Manhattan
Water Company; another in New York employed in a saw
mill; two in Philadelphia, owned by the city, to supply
water and to power a rolling and slitting mill; and one in
Boston used in some manufacture. All but one of these had
been put into operation since the turn of the century.

The fates of John Fitch and Oliver Evans were indicative
of the conservative attitude most Americans held when
confronted by technological innovations. In 1789 Fitch
invented a successful steamboat which plied the waters of
the Delaware around Philadelphia through that summer.
The public, however, gave little support to Fitch, and the
company which he had founded to commercialize his invention failed. Undaunted, Fitch built a better boat driven
by a screw propeller. But this too met with scant financial
backing in either Philadelphia or New York. A similar fate

was experienced when Fitch tried to introduce his steamboat into western waters in Kentucky. By now thoroughly dejected, Fitch turned first to the bottle and then to opium. He was found dead one morning in 1798 in an obscure Kentucky inn after an overdose of drugs.

Evans' story, while not so melodramatic, is similarly suggestive of popular attitudes. Oliver Evans was one of American's foremost mechanical geniuses, easily the equal of the more celebrated Eli Whitney. As early as 1772, while a wagon-maker's apprentice, he had considered steam-driven carriages feasible. In 1787 he obtained from the Maryland legislature the exclusive right to make and use steam wagons within that state for fourteen years. But Evans found no capitalists who were willing to risk the few thousand dollars that he felt necessary for his experiments. Even the engineer and later steamboat promoter Benjamin Latrobe, in an 1803 report to the American Philosophical Society, called Evans' ideas absurd. Evans then tried to raise the money by offering a standing bet of $3000 that he could build a steam-driven wagon able "to run upon a level road against the swiftest horse." He found no takers and eventually abandoned the project. In 1812 he resignedly wrote in *Niles' Register:* "When we reflect upon the obstinate opposition that has been made by a great majority to every step towards improvement . . . it is too much to expect the monstrous leap from bad roads to railways and steam carriages, at once."

Yet changes were occurring by 1812 when Evans made these observations, and he, in part, was responsible for introducing technological improvements that were moving America toward a more mechanized, affluent, and hectic future. Early in his career Evans had revolutionized the flour-milling industry by inventing numerous grain-handling machines, including an elevator, a conveyor, a descender, and a hopper-boy. During the 1780's Evans' mill in Philadelphia was so organized that grain was mechanically conveyed through the building while other devices cleaned, ground, cooled, bolted, and barrelled it. His *Young Mill-Wright & Miller's Guide* (1795) went through many editions, and within a generation most major mills had adopted his machinery. During this same period Evans became increasingly interested in steam power, and, although his plans for a steam carriage met with little enthusiasm, his development of a high pressure stationary steam engine was to have a major impact. After establishing the Mars Iron Works in 1807, Evans built about fifty engines. He also constructed for the city of Philadelphia the first steam dredge in America in 1805. Called the *Orukter Amphibolos,* Evans' dredge was indeed amphibious and was driven to the docks under its own steam and with much ceremony.

Other innovators such as Eli Whitney and Robert Fulton were having a similar impact. Though most famous for his invention of the cotton gin in 1793, which during the early nineteenth century was a factor in the expansion of cotton-capitalism and slavery through the lower South, Whitney made an equally significant contribution by the introduction of modern mass production based on interchangeable parts. French experiments along these lines had greatly impressed Thomas Jefferson as early as 1785; however, both the French and the British had abandoned the scheme as having too many practical difficulties. With the support of a government contract for 10,000 muskets, Whitney perfected this system. In 1800 at a Washington demonstration before the Secretary of War and other government officials, Whitney won influential support for mass production by assembling ten perfectly fitted muskets from random piles of identical parts. But the real key to making the principle of interchangeable parts practical was the development of machinery which could turn out preci-

sion parts. Whitney designed and built many machines of
this nature in the early years of the century. Within a
generation, not only firearms, but clocks and watches as
well, were being produced by what Europeans came to call
"the American system."

Like Evans and Whitney, Robert Fulton was a many-
faceted mechanical genius. An expert gunsmith during the
Revolution, Fulton turned to portrait and landscape painting in the years after the war. Gaining recognition but little
else, he abandoned art and took up canal engineering and
the invention of machinery. For several years he worked
on such devices as underwater torpedoes and submarines,
and perfected a self-propelled submarine mine. In 1802 he
contracted to build a steamboat with Robert R. Livingston,
who held a monopoly for steamboat navigation on the
Hudson. Fulton designed the *Clermont,* a boat with two
side paddlewheels powered by an English engine. On August 17, 1807, the *Clermont* began a successful first voyage
from New York to Albany and back which was completed
in the then rapid time of five days. Although American
prejudices against steam travel did not end overnight,
nevertheless, within a few years steamboats were regularly
plying the Hudson, the Delaware, and other eastern
waterways. In 1811 the Fulton-Livingston group, which had
obtained monopoly privileges from the Territory of Orleans,
successfully sent the Pittsburgh-built steamboat, the *New
Orleans,* down the Ohio and Mississippi. By 1817 steamboats were fast becoming a familiar sight on western rivers
and lakes.

Yet despite the individual inventive genius of such persons as Evans, Whitney, and Fulton, the widespread acceptance of mechanized industry and transportation might
well have lagged for many years had it not been for the
external circumstances that substantially cut the United
States off from Europe between 1807 and 1815. Deprived

of imports by the restrictive legislation of Jefferson and Madison, and blockaded by Britain following the outbreak of war in 1812, Americans were forced to manufacture their own commodities. Many wealthy merchants and shippers, suffering from the decline of trade, turned to manufacturing. The famous Lowell system was begun in 1813 when a former Boston merchant, Francis Cabot Lowell, established at Waltham the first textile factory to conduct all the operations for turning cotton into cloth by power under a single roof. By the end of the War of 1812 the factory system had a foothold, and, although manufacturing would suffer some setbacks due to heavy English importations after 1815 and the depression of 1819, America would never again be the almost exclusively agrarian society it had been in the early years of the nineteenth century.

The war years had not only been a spur to industry; they had also helped alter American attitudes, convincing many persons that true independence could come only if the nation were economically self-sufficient and had an adequate system of transportation. The spirit of nationalism that swept the country after 1815 helped sustain this sentiment. In 1816 Congress responded by passing a protective tariff and chartering the second Bank of the United States. Congress also approved a bill the following year to provide federal funds for road construction, but this was vetoed by President Madison on constitutional grounds.

Despite presidential scruples, however, internal improvements were being advanced at a rapid pace. The early success of the Lancaster turnpike in the 1790's had given rise to a boom in road building, particularly in New England and the Middle States. Construction of the federally financed National Road from Baltimore began in 1811 and by 1818 had been completed across the mountains to Wheeling on the Ohio River, making easier the settlement and development of the West. In 1817 the New York Legislature, following the advice of Governor DeWitt Clinton, authorized construction of a canal to connect the Hudson to the Great Lakes. Completed in October, 1825, the Erie Canal ran over 350 miles from Albany to Buffalo and quickly proved profitable because it created both an easy route for western emigration and a means of transporting goods cheaply and efficiently. Its success started a canal-building craze throughout the nation.

Enthusiastic support for rapid transportation became widespread. By the mid-1820's Mathew Carey, the Philadelphia publisher, economist, and social reformer, had little difficulty in getting hundreds of persons to join a Society for the Promotion of Internal Improvements with an initiation fee of $100 "to finance the dissemination of accurate information on canals, roads, bridges, railways, and steam engines." As a reporter for the *United States Gazette,* February 23, 1825, wrote: "One hundred dollars, the highest initiatory fee that we recollect in our country, are demanded as the price of the privilege of serving their country in its ranks, with the certainty, that this bread cast upon the waters, can return but after many days, and *that only* in the consciousness of having been useful to others."

The early revolutions in industry and transportation had a marked effect on the American population, and did a great deal to eliminate the idleness that Henry Adams had described as characteristic at the turn of the century. George White, a staunch advocate of manufacturing and an early biographer of Samuel Slater, commented on just this change. "In districts far from markets," he wrote, men "are too apt, for want of due encouragement to industrious habits, to throw away their time in worse than useless idleness and dissipation. Whoever has experienced the difficulties attendant on almost all efforts for the moral advancement of a poor and scattered population, without this encouragement, and compares them with the facilities afforded by thriving towns and villages, inhabited and surrounded by an industrious and happy people, will see at once that whatever tends to improve the physical condition of man, must, as it renders him more comfortable, conduce, in no small degree, to the improvement of his morals . . . ."

By the time of Jackson's presidency an idle American was a rarity. Foreign travelers and native writers alike attest to the fact that haste had become a national characteristic. Returning from Europe in 1836, the sculptor Horatio Greenough saw speed as the key to American character. "Rail Roads alone seem to be *understood*," he observed. "Go ahead! is the order of the day. The whole continent presents a scene of *scrabbling* and roars with greedy hurry." "Life consists in motion," testified Francis Grund, an Austrian who had settled in America in the late 1820's. "The United States present certainly the most animated picture of universal bustle and activity of any country in the world. Such a thing as rest or quiescence does not even enter the mind of an American . . . . This state of incessant excitement gives to the American an air of busy inquietude . . . which, in fact, constitutes their principle happiness."

Grund went on to note that "the position of a man of leisure in the United States is far from being enviable; for . . . he is not only left without companions to enjoy his luxuriant ease, but, what is worse, he forfeits the respect of his fellow citizens, who, by precept and example are determined to discountenance idleness." Even the little leisure that was allowed seemed to be taken up with nervous activity; American rocking, whittling, and chewing continually amazed foreign visitors.

Another seeming change in American values was the new openness with which persons came to accept technological[2] innovations. While in the United States in the 1820's,

Frederick List, the German economist, observed that "everything new is quickly introduced here, and all the latest inventions. There is no clinging to old ways, the moment an American hears the word 'invention' he pricks up his ears." "The inventors of machinery," stated the New York author James Kirke Paulding in the late 1820's, "have caused a greater revolution in the habits, opinions, and morals of mankind, than all the efforts of legislation. Machinery and steam engines have had more influence on the Christian world than Locke's metaphysics, Napoleon's code, or Jeremy Bentham's codification." Machinery, in the words of Salmon P. Chase in 1832, has "freed the inherent energy of moral ideas, removed obstructions out of the way of their action, and has brought them into contact with the objects on which they are to act." That same year a writer for the *North American Review* declared: "What we claim for machinery is, that it is in modern times by far the most efficient physical cause of human improvement; that it does for civilization what conquest and human labor formerly did, and accomplishes incalculably more than they accomplished." Five years later, Edward Everett, then governor of Massachusetts, exclaimed: "The mechanician, not the magician, is now the master of life." "Are not our inventors," asked another enthusiast, "absolutely ushering in the very dawn of the millennium?"

Even air transportation enticed the innovative individuals of this new age. American aeronautics could be said to date from 1830. On September 9 of that year Charles Ferson Durant, the first of many pre-Civil War "aeronauts," ascended in a balloon from New York City's Castle Garden at the tip of the Battery. A reported 20,000 persons watched Durant clear the castle battlements and drift

[2] Fittingly the term "technology" was of Jacksonian origin. It was first given popular currency with the 1829 publication of a book entitled *Elements of Technology* by Jacob Bigelow, Harvard's first Rumford professor "of the application of science to the art of living."

skyward out over Staten Island. Fearing he might blow out to sea, Durant descended before a small but impressed crowd at Perth Amboy, New Jersey, having come some thirty miles in about an hour.

Within a few years balloon ascents had become popular spectator events throughout the nation. On one occasion in June, 1833, both President Jackson and the celebrated Indian chief Black Hawk appeared at another Durant ascension from Castle Garden. "At an early hour," reported the *New York Daily Advertiser,* "the Garden was filled; the Battery wharves, piers and houses appeared black with people. The water being undisturbed, the bay appeared almost covered with steamboats, sailboats, and every other description of water craft, all filled with people. To say that a hundred thousand witnessed the ascension, from various parts, would be a small computation."

As might be expected, Black Hawk and his fellow Indians were astonished by the balloon flight. "We had seen many wonderful sights on our way," the chief proclaimed in his dictated autobiography published the following year, "large villages, the great *national road* over the mountains, the *rail roads,* steam carriages, ships, steam boats, and many other things; but we were now about to witness a sight more surprising than any of these. We were told that a man was going up into the air in a balloon! We watched with anxiety to see if it could be true; and to our astonishment, saw him ascend in the air until our eyes could no longer perceive him."

But to the bustling Americans of the mid-thirties such phenomena were becoming almost commonplace. In 1835 Richard Clayton, a young English immigrant who had settled in Cincinnati, established a long-distance balloon world record by flying from that city to Monroe County, Virginia, covering the distance of some 350 miles in a brisk nine and a half hours. A few months later Clayton experimented, though unsuccessfully, with airmail service. Even a patent for a propeller-driven plane was taken out by a Baltimore inventor John H. Pennington in 1838. Little wonder then that thousands of persons readily believed the astounding account published in the *New York Sun,* April 13, 1844, of a three-day Atlantic crossing completed by eight aeronauts in "Mr. Monck Mason's Flying Machine." The story, of course, was an Edgar Allan Poe hoax.

Another reflection of American willingness to break with past traditions was the emergence in this period of what John Kouwenhoven has described as the "vernacular style"—a simple, unadorned functionalism. This can be seen in such things as farm machinery, bridges, steamboats, and locomotives. In constructing these, American designers were much more willing than Europeans to sacrifice the old for the new. The location of the machinery, noted an English engineer in the 1830's, forms "one of the most prominent and striking parts of an American steamboat . . . , presenting, as may naturally be supposed, a strange effect in the eyes of those accustomed to see European steam-boats only, in which no part of the machinery is visible even from the deck of the vessel." To grasp the greater willingness of American designers to create new forms for new functions, one has only to compare John Stevens' 1825 locomotive or Cyrus McCormick's first reaper (1831) with such English inventions as Samuel Gurney's 1827 steam carriage. The latter, though technically advanced, is clearly designed in the style of a traditional upper-class carriage; both Stevens' and McCormick's inventions, on the other hand, make no attempt to disguise their functions. The best of American industrial art, contended a patent commissioner, is that in which "the form and proportion of every implement or dwelling has a close relation to its purpose."

As Americans became more innovative and less idle, they

developed a new sense of progress. The idea of progress, of course, was not unique to the 1820's and 1830's. Many Americans of the eighteenth century believed strongly in the possibilities of progress. This was a basic tenet of Enlightenment thought, and for many persons the success of the American Revolution was vivid proof of mankind's advance. Yet for most eighteenth-century Americans, whether they viewed progress in material terms or in a more idealistic sense, the amelioration of mankind was felt to be a slow process. Furthermore, numerous doubts remained concerning the nature of man and the improvability of society. The debates at the Constitutional Convention in 1787, where even the most liberal delegates expressed certain reservations about man's innate goodness, make this quite clear.

By the late 1820's, however, doubts about progress had all but disappeared, and not only was human betterment believed possible, it was also expected to be rapid. As the historian John Thomas has pointed out, this was part of a broader change from the rational outlook of the Enlightenment to the emotional attitude associated with Romanticism. "A romantic religious faith," Thomas writes, "had changed an Enlightenment doctrine of progress into a dynamic principle of reform." The concept of progress had come to mean romantic perfectionism which demanded immediate improvement. This was reflected in such seemingly diverse Jacksonian phenomena as the President's attack on the Bank, Garrison's advocacy of immediate abolition of slavery, William Miller's prediction of an imminent millennium, and the ordinary citizen's rising material aspirations.

Another historian, Stow Persons, has described this change from the late eighteenth century to the 1820's in terms of theories of history. Persons contends that most American thinkers of the Revolutionary period, including

John Adams and Thomas Jefferson, held a cyclical view of history. Nations were thought to have natural life cycles analogous to living organisms. America after the Revolution, it was believed, was in a state of youth which made it morally superior to Europe. Safeguards were needed to bolster the new nation's youthful virtue, however, since, as Jefferson warned in 1781, "the spirit of the times may alter, will alter. Our rulers will become corrupt, our people careless. A single zealot may commence persecuter, and better men be his victims." America's enviable position was precarious and ultimately likely to dissipate. Its continuance depended on preserving moral virtues, which for Jefferson meant maintaining an agrarian way of life.

Gradually, however, in the early nineteenth century the cyclical theory came to seem less relevant to Americans; it became more common to see this nation's history in terms of progress alone. Suggestive of this changing view were Jefferson's thoughts on history in his latter years. "Science," he wrote to John Adams, October 28, 1813, "had liberated the ideas of those who read and reflect, and the American example had kindled feelings of right in the people. An insurrection has consequently begun, of science, talents and courage against rank and birth, which have fallen into contempt . . . . Science is progressive, and talents and enterprise on the alert." Even the more conservative Adams in old age also abandoned the cyclical theory in favor of progressive belief. Writing to Jefferson in 1821 he stated: "You and I hope for splendid improvements in human society, and vast amelioration in the condition of mankind. Our faith may be supported by more rational arguments than any former. I own that I am very sanguine in the belief of them as I hope and believe you are . . . ." The changing views of Jefferson and Adams, remarkable in their own right for men of that age, mirrored those of society generally, and by the 1820's, as Persons concludes, the idea of progress had become "the fighting faith of men with a mission to perform, whether to feed the hungry, convert the heathen, or accumulate one's pile."

The strong faith in progress tended to make Americans always slightly dissatisfied with the present but expectant of a better future. "It is peculiarly the happy privilege of Americans," stated William James, a wealthy New York contractor and grandfather of the philosopher and the novelist, "to enjoy the blessings of hope and expectation." The expectations most commonly shared by Jacksonian Americans were unquestionably economic. " *'Go ahead'* is the real motto of the country," proclaimed a foreign traveler, "and every man does push on, to gain in advance of his neighbour." Alexis de Tocqueville was struck by the fact that "it is not only a portion of the people which is busied with the amelioration of its social condition, but the whole community is engaged in the task." "How widely spread," noted William Ellery Channing, "is the passion for acquisition, not for simple subsistence, but for wealth! What a rush into all departments of trade."

Given the passion for wealth that dominated most Americans, it is not surprising to find that this era gave rise to the cult of the "self-made man."[3] Journalists, clergymen, lawyers, and others reiterated that anything was possible. Jackson himself, an orphan and clearly self-made, was a fitting symbol for the age. Examples of persons inspired to new aspirations by the rags-to-riches philosophy are many. Thomas Mellon, the founder of that family's fortune, recalled that as a young man of fourteen in 1828 he had been motivated by the dream of economic betterment through reading the classic American success story Franklin's *Autobiography.* "I had not before imagined," Mellon wrote, "any other course of life superior to farming,

---

[3] The term "self-made man" was first coined, according to the historian of this subject, Irvin Wyllie, by Henry Clay in 1832.

but the reading of Franklin's life led me to question this view. For so poor and friendless a boy to be able to become a merchant or a professional man had before seemed an impossibility; but here was Franklin poorer than myself, who by industry, thrift and frugality had become learned and wise, and elevated to wealth and fame." Mellon soon left the family farm at Poverty Point and moved to nearby Pittsburgh where he quickly advanced as a lawyer, money lender, and finally banker.

That Mellon's quest for fortune led him from farm to city was not unusual for the age. Although agriculture remained the leading economic pursuit through the pre-Civil War period, ambitious Americans like Mellon were turning to more rapidly rewarding occupations in such fields as commerce and manufacturing. "My disposition," wrote a young man in 1818, "would not allow me to work on a farm . . . . I thought that I Should be one of the happiest fellows in the world If I could only be rich, and I thought as others had begun with nothin and become men of fortune that I might . . . ." Tocqueville noted the trend away from farming. "The cultivation of the ground," he wrote, "promises an almost certain result of his [the farmer's] exertions, but a slow one . . . . Agriculture is therefore only suited to those who have already large superfluous wealth, or to those whose penury bids them seek only a bare subsistence . . . . Thus democracy leads men to prefer one kind of labour to another; and whilst it diverts them from agriculture, it encourages their taste for commerce and manufactures."

One result of the rising economic expectations and consequent attractiveness of nonagrarian pursuits was the great urban growth of the era. Up to about 1820 the expansion of cities had been slow at best. In fact America had a larger percentage of urban dwellers in relation to the total population in 1700 (ca. ten per cent) than a century later when about six per cent of the people could be classified as urban. The rate of urbanization picked up slightly between 1800 and 1810, reaching 7.3 per cent by the latter date. But in the next decade, westward expansion and lack of immigration actually caused the city population to increase at a slightly slower rate than the population generally, and by 1820 only 7.2 per cent of the people lived in cities. The decade of the twenties, however, reversed this trend and began the rapid urbanization of the nation which would be so significant in differentiating modern America from its rural past. By 1830 approximately ten per cent of Americans were city dwellers. By 1860 this percentage had doubled in the most rapid period of urban growth in the nation's history. Between 1820 and 1840 Philadelphia and its immediate suburbs had grown from about 100,000 to well over 200,000; Pittsburgh during these same decades went from slightly over 7,000 to more than 21,000; New York, America's major metropolis, swelled from 123,000 to over 312,000 in these twenty years; while cities such as Lowell and Chicago which had not existed prior to 1820 were fast becoming major centers. In short, the rise of the modern city has been a fairly recent phenomenon beginning about the age of Jackson.

Rapid urbanization, improved transportation, industrialization, new technological innovations, westward expansion, increased mobility, rising aspirations, and greater wealth were rapidly altering American society during the 1820's and 1830's. By the time Jackson assumed the presidency, America appeared young, buoyant, and expanding. Optimism was widespread. The nation presents a "scene of unmingled prosperity and happiness," declared a Jacksonian Fourth of July orator. The ordinary citizen, he continued, has "his aspirations lifted up to the most exalted objects . . . ." "It has been seen," wrote Mathew Carey in his 1829 *Essay on Wages,* "that the United States are comparatively free from those disturbing causes which impede the growth of capital. With a vast body of land; with mines of gold, lead, iron, copper, and coal, abounding in every direction; circulating capital alone was wanting to bring them into activity, and the system has tended to promote its rapid growth. Secure in person and property, comparatively free from taxation, unrestrained in action, comparatively so in all matters of trade, and very industrious, the people of this country, applying their labour in the way which they think will produce the largest reward, find their capital rapidly augmented; the consequence of which is, that mines are opened in all directions, new lands are brought into cultivation, rail-roads and canals are constructed, and machinery is applied in every way to increase the produce of labour. Capital flows from all quarters to this country, where it can be best paid for, and, increasing the demand for labour, finds employment, not only for the vast natural increase in population, but for great numbers who are led to seek here an improvement of their condition."

So abundant and promising did the future seem that most American economists, whether free-traders or protectionists, rejected the gloomy theories of Thomas Malthus. Hezekiah Niles, the indefatigable publisher of *Niles' Weekly Register,* held that in the United States the population, far from being excessive and a cause of poverty, constituted "the strength and wealth of our country . . . ." Henry Carey, the son of Mathew Carey and one of this country's most original economists, wrote in 1835: "Mr. Malthus tells us, that wherever food is abundant, population increases rapidly; but it might be correctly said, that where population increases rapidly, food is abundant, and we have full evidence that with increased population, the dangers of famine are greatly decreased, where man is not too much trammeled."

Yet American optimism, real though it was, was not the only sentiment prevalent. This was also a time of tensions and insecurities. The speed of social and economic change in these years could not help but generate uncertainties. Prior to 1815, America had been a fairly stable society for nearly two centuries; except for the Revolution, changes had occurred gradually and within accustomed institutional frameworks. After that date, however, new technology, new forms of economic organization, and newly enriched persons presented a challenge to the old certitudes. The traditional moral values were not always consonant with the emerging practices of American capitalism. Restlessness and inner tensions resulted. The look of alienation on Rip Van Winkle's face as painted by John Quidor was indeed representative of a growing attitude which many Americans shared in confronting the changing social scene. Subsequent chapters will examine in more detail some of the underlying anxieties and tensions in Jacksonian America.

CHAPTER TWO

"In Time, Again to be Deposed"

AS THE FIRST WESTERN STEAMBOAT, THE *New Orleans,* churned down the Ohio and Mississippi Rivers in 1811, Indians fled from the banks. Just above the mouth of the Ohio some emboldened Chickasaws gave chase in a large canoe. For a time the primitive craft nearly overtook the steamboat, but the endurance of steam power soon proved too much, and with wild shouts the Indians gave up pursuit and returned to the forest. It was later learned that the Indians called the steamboat "Penelore," or "fire Canoe," and that they linked it in their minds both with a bright comet that had been visible just before the ship's arrival and with a spectacular earthquake which was sending severe tremors down the Ohio and Mississippi valleys just as the ship appeared. To persons not accustomed to any of these events their coincidence seemed apocalyptic.

The most severe damage caused by the earthquake was at the small village of New Madrid on the western bank of the Mississippi in the later state of Missouri. There the ground had opened in great chasms, destroying houses and killing several inhabitants. When the *New Orleans* landed at this town shortly after the disaster, terror-stricken survivors begged to be taken on board but were refused; others, dreading the steamboat even more than the earthquake, ran off in panic. Even on board the dignitaries making this maiden voyage were fearful as modern machinery penetrated America's wilderness. One of the passengers, Mrs. Nicholas Roosevelt, noted an ominous silence on the trip except for the fiery engine. "No one seemed disposed to talk; and when there was any conversation, it was carried on in whispers . . . ." Even the ship's dog was uneasy and "prowled about, moaning and growling." Mrs. Roosevelt reported that she "lived in constant fright, unable to sleep or sew, or read." For some, then, the first steamboat on western waters—a traditional symbol of progress through technology—was an omen of evil.

Until recently historians, in evaluating the course of American history from the War of 1812 through the 1840's, have based their interpretations upon the doctrine of progress. Since these were years of incredible economic and geographical expansion, such an interpretation was easy to support, and the innumerable booster writings of the period seemed to give such a view ample documentation. The obvious doubters—the Thoreaus, Poes, Hawthornes, and Melvilles—were explained away as an eccentric but minor dissonance in the otherwise harmonious chorus of hope. They became the "nay sayers" of textbook terminology, filling a page or two with their bizarre gloom in a narrative of otherwise nearly uninterrupted optimism.

In recent years, however, scholars have uncovered convincing evidence of widespread uneasiness in expanding young America. The apprehension which greeted the first steamboat on western waters was not unique. During the fifty years following this event there was a great deal of disquiet expressed concerning the real meaning of America's materialistic, mechanical, and geographic expansion. While sometimes this vexation was voiced as a direct challenge to the whole concept of progress, it more often took the form of covert fears underlying and clouding a progressive vision. Historians today undoubtedly have a greater affinity for these undercurrents and tensions in Jacksonian America since present-day society is experiencing somewhat similar anxieties in the face of rapid innovations. It now appears axiomatic that major economic, social, and political changes, however beneficial they might appear in retrospect, cannot help but create insecurities in the society that is experiencing them.

While adjustment to rapid change is never easy, it was made more difficult for the Jacksonian generation because the changes being wrought were without precedent. When Jefferson in his first Inaugural Address (1801) remarked that the nation, bounded to the west by the Mississippi, contained "room enough for our descendants to the hundreth and thousandth generation," he was reflecting the thinking of a people used to slow change. Yet by the 1820's, not only had steam power penetrated these western lands, but actual settlement had already pushed beyond the Mississippi itself. Factories and machines were altering American economic organization, and, perhaps more significantly, were changing people's values.

As American society changed, social cohesion was threatened. Industry, immigration, and expansion were creating a pluralistic society; yet many persons clung to a single-track vision of what the country should be. That the unfamiliar alarmed Americans is evidenced by the bitter attacks against such groups as Catholics, Masons, or Mormons. Scapegoats were common. Villains ranged from alcoholics to atheists, bankers to slave holders, anarchists to monarchists. Change itself was suspect; James Fenimore Cooper, whose writings mirrored many of America's anxieties, had a character remark despairingly: "the whole country is in such a constant state of mutation, that I can only liken it to the game of children, in which, as one quits his corner another runs into it, and he that finds no corner to get into, is the laughing-stock of the others."

Surprisingly, one of the chief causes of consternation was the very material success of the American economy. The notion that morality thrived best on adversity was a common belief embedded in Protestant thought. Timothy Flint, the New England clergyman, on viewing fashionable Saratoga Springs in the mid-1820's after extended travels through the Ohio Valley, noted that "here there is brought, full in your view, the great change, which the American character has recently undergone. A lover of the country cannot but regret to see that we are making such rapid strides in extravagance and luxury." Flint's feeling that fashionable living had undermined the virtues of hard work and had turned Americans toward a gambling, get-rich-quick scramble for money was echoed increasingly from the 1820's through the Civil War years. The Reverend Elihu Baldwin of New York, preaching in 1827, warned that "increasing wealth rolls the tide of fashionable vice over the land. Who that reflects, but must tremble for the consequences?" "The inordinate pursuit of money," Reverend Caleb Stetson declared in 1842, "for the gratification of avarice, vanity, pride, and ambition, has deeply corrupted the principles of the country, and nearly destroyed all generous public feeling." This is "the age of gaudy wealth," claimed a disapproving Episcopal Bishop in the 1850's. "Wealth came in and created social distinction which took the place of family, and thus society became vulgarized."

Not only ministers, but laymen as well were disturbed by the seeming changes prosperity had wrought on American character. One of the most persistent critics of American materialism was the novelist Cooper. In his first venture into social commentary in the mid-twenties, Cooper had staunchly defended this country against European criticisms. His *Notions of the Americans* (1828) painted an Arcadian picture of a settled and virtuous farming people content with hard work and simple pleasures. His ideal was a middle ground between the extremes of wilderness and civilization, embodying the best of both. A natural yet democratic aristocracy led this stable, orderly society.

An extended stay in Europe followed by a return to the aggressively materialistic America of the 1830's caused Cooper to realize how far his *Notions of the Americans* was from reality; he changed from defender of his countrymen to critic. There exists no more biting caricature of the money-grubbing man-on-the-make in all of American literature than Cooper's depiction of Aristabulus Bragg in *Home as Found* (1838)—a novel that contrasted American realities with his earlier ideal. Bragg was described as "quick-witted, prompt in action, enterprising in all things in which he has nothing to lose, but wary and cautious in all things in which he has a real stake, and ready to turn not only his hand, but his heart and his principles, to anything that offers an advantage. With him, literally, 'Nothing is too high to be aspired to, nothing too low to be done' .... Such a compound of shrewdness, impudence, common-sense, pretension, humility, cleverness, vulgarity, kind-heartedness, duplicity, selfishness, law-honesty, moral fraud and mother wit, mixed up with a smattering of learning and much penetration in practical things, can hardly be described, as any one of his prominent qualities is certain to be met by another quite as obvious that is almost its converse. Mr. Bragg, in short, is purely a creature of circumstances, his qualities pointing him out for either a member of Congress or a deputy sheriff, offices that he is equally ready to fill."

Bragg epitomized the go-ahead American. For him all

was expectation; he had no sense of history, and no attachment to home or place. When asked if he did not have a favorite tree, he replied: "I have found some trees much pleasanter than others, and the pleasantest tree I can remember was one of my own, out of which the sawyers made a thousand feet of clear stuff, to say nothing of middlings." He was astonished to learn that in England a highway, canal, or railway was "obliged to make a curve to avoid a churchyard or a tombstone."

Cooper's judgment of Bragg and his type was well summed up by John Effingham, the fictional spokesman for the author's position in *Home as Found*. On showing Wall Street to an English friend, Effingham remarked that here "all principles are swallowed up in the absorbing desire for gain—national honor, permanent security, the ordinary rules of society, law, the constitution, and everything that is usually so dear to men, are forgotten, or are perverted in order to sustain this unnatural condition of things . . . . The entire community," he continued, "is in the situation of a man who is in the incipient stages of an exhilarating intoxication, and who keeps pouring down glass after glass, in the idle notion he is merely sustaining nature in her ordinary functions."

Effingham's charge that wealth gained through means other than hard labor was unnatural was one that appeared frequently in the writings and rhetoric of the era. Labor leaders, politicians, clergymen, and others not only claimed that speculative riches were a violation of nature, they also charged that such ill-begotten wealth weakened the nation's moral fiber. The image of a people becoming effeminant through luxury appears again and again. "Will you tell me," asked John Adams of Jefferson in 1819, "how to prevent riches from producing luxury? Will you tell me how to prevent luxury from producing effeminacy intoxication extravagance Vice and Folly?" Sudden wealth, contended

Samuel Putnam Waldo, an early biographer of Jackson, created "voluptuousness and effeminacy" and rapidly diminished "that exalted sense of national glory." "The old hearts of oak are gone," lamented Horace Mann in 1842. "Society is suffering under a curvature of the spine . . . . There is a general effeminacy of our modes of life, as compared with the indurating exposures of our ancestors."

Only a return to orthodox Protestantism, believed many of that persuasion, could save America from the perils of its own prosperity. Lyman Beecher, an influential spokesman for such a position, declared in 1829: "The greater our prosperity the shorter its duration, and the more tremendous our downfall, unless the moral power of the Gospel shall be exerted to arrest those causes which have destroyed other nations . . . . Our Republic is becoming too prosperous, too powerful, too extended, too numerous, to be governed by any power without the blessed influence of the Gospel." In 1843, the executive committee of the American Tract Society contended that the very survival of the country depended on evangelical Protestantism. Condemning freedom of the press as leading to "unbridled licentiousness," freedom of immigration as undermining the political system and aiding the "spiritual despotism" of Catholicism, the committee concluded that only when there existed an "absolute dependence on the spirit of God" would the nation be safe.

Even specific national crises were attributed to affluence. Edward G. Prescott, speaking in Boston on the nullification crisis of 1833, stated: "Our Country presents a situation hitherto unparallelled among men. We are suffering, not like the nations of Europe from a debt which bows us to the earth under our vain efforts to discharge it, but from a state of prosperity which is perhaps even worse." Similarly Emerson, after the passage of the Fugitive Slave Law, claimed that "our prosperity had hurt us" since we were not shocked by this crime.

The strongest charge leveled by the critics of wealth was that it jeopardized the Republic itself. Emma Willard, for instance, addressing the New York State Legislature to seek aid for the establishment of female seminaries, spoke of women's education as a means of preserving "among females of wealthy families, that purity of manners, which is . . . so necessary to the existence of a republican government." Under existing conditions, she warned, America's republican institutions were threatened by too much wealth and its resultant "luxuries and follies." "It may be said, that the depravation of morals and manners, can be traced to the introduction of wealth, as its cause." She was particularly concerned because "females have been exposed to the contagion of wealth without the preservation of a good education." Wealthy women "have erected the idol fashion; and upon her altar, they sacrifice, with shameless rites, whatever is sacred to virtue or religion."

The aged Jefferson, in a letter to William B. Giles, December 26, 1825, saw a danger that moneyed men might change the very structure of government in the interest of those "who, having nothing in them of the feelings or principles of '76, now look to a single and splendid government of an aristocracy, founded on banking institutions, and moneyed incorporations under the guise and cloak of their favored branches of manufactures, commerce and navigation, riding and ruling over the plundered ploughman and beggared yeomanry." Such a charge would become central a few years later in the rhetoric of Jacksonian Democrats and labor leaders.

Anxieties over America's affluence were intensified in the Jacksonian generation because of the vague notion that this material success was somehow at variance with the nation's past. Jefferson's reference to the "principles of '76" conjured up an image of selfless heroes sacrificing personal gain for higher national ideals. George Bancroft's popular *History of the United States,* the first volume of which went through ten editions between 1834 and 1844, was a moral tract attacking such traits as "avarice," "covetousness," "greediness," and "passion for gain"; while holding up for emulation values reflecting altruistic benevolence—"self-denial," "disinterested conduct," "no slave to avarice." Fourth of July orations almost invariably conveyed a similar message. The popularity of this view of the past reflected the uneasiness persons felt when confronting the competitive and materialistic present; the contrast between this romanticized past and the existing realities, however, served only to intensify disquietude.

One method of avoiding the contrast between an heroic and ascetic past and the prosperous and indulgent present was to depict such prosperity as the natural outgrowth of the republican institutions initiated by the Revolutionary generation. For a time, the bridge between past and present was made easier by the continuance in power of persons closely associated with the Revolutionary era. The first five presidents—Washington, Adams, Jefferson, Madison, and Monroe—were all linked in men's minds with the Revolution and as long as they were on the scene it was easier to see the present as the natural offspring of the past. Their passing made this more difficult. By the time Monroe left office in 1825, the age of the Founding Fathers had clearly passed and political power rested with the generation of Clay, Calhoun, Webster, and John Qunicy Adams.

Yet there were still ways in which the men of the past could be used to serve the present. Lafayette's triumphal return and tour of America in 1824–25 was a good example. Fred Somkin in a recent study considers this visit "a cultural event of tremendous magnitude which involved all sections of the nation and the participation of Americans in all stations of life. As such, it offered a marvelously unified setting . . . in which to identify and track down a host of fascinating clues, all pointing toward a determined and almost desperate American attempt to justify the present and the future through a time-defying union with the virtuous past." Lafayette's forty-year absence from America made him seem a figure from the grave resurrected to bestow the blessings of a simpler age on the bustling world of steam and slavery. Everywhere he traveled he was called on to praise the prosperous present and to assure Americans that this well-being was an "authentic derivation of the past of the Founding Fathers."

Less than a year following Lafayette's departure another event occurred which seemed to assure Americans that their present was guided by divine providence and directly connected with their heroic history. On July 4, 1826, the fiftieth anniversary of American independence, Thomas Jefferson and John Adams died within five hours of one another. Such a wondrous coincidence, declared Adams' son, President John Quincy Adams, in his official proclamation, gave concrete assurance that the work of these two founders was "Heaven directed." Providence, declared Edward Everett, "seems to have appointed that the revolutionary age of America should be closed, by a scene as illustriously affecting, as its commencement was appalling and terrific." Jefferson himself, only ten days before he died, had written a speech to be read on the Fourth which became something of a valedictory following the dramatic coincidence of his and Adams' deaths. "All eyes are opened, or opening, to the rights of man," he had written. "The general spread of the light of science has already laid open to every view the palpable truth, that the mass of mankind has not been born with saddles on their backs, nor a favored few booted and spurred, ready to ride them legitimately, by the grace of God." Reprinted in newspapers across the country, engraved and framed as a souvenir, this last testament of Jefferson's, with its celebration of science and human progress, was taken to mean that the Declaration of Independence was being fulfilled in America.

By 1828, the year of Jackson's first election to the presidency, there survived only one signer of the Declaration, Charles Carroll of Carrollton; he too became a significant symbol who tied the ideals of the Revolution to the new age of steam. On July 4, 1828, in what *Niles' Register* described as "the most splendid civic procession, perhaps, ever exhibited in America" the citizens of Baltimore celebrated the beginnings of the nation's first railroad. Fifty thousand persons lined the streets as Carroll, the guest of honor, and other dignitaries paraded by. In his speech the aged signer performed his symbolic duty well: "I consider this among the most important acts of my life, second only to my signing of the Declaration of Independence, if even it be second to that."

As the generation of the founders passed from the scene in the twenties and thirties, Americans tried various means of commemorating and preserving their sense of the past. The era witnessed something of an historical revival that began perhaps as early as 1820 with the consecration of Plymouth Rock. Speaking on that commemorative occasion, Daniel Webster declared that Americans of the present were "allied to our ancestors; allied to our posterity; closely compacted on all sides with others; ourselves being but links in the great chain of being, which begins with the origin of our race, runs onward through its successive generations, binding together the past, the present, and the future." Five years later Lafayette laid the cornerstone of the Bunker Hill Monument. During these same years Jared Sparks was collecting historical documents and editing the papers of Washington; historical societies were being established in various parts of the country. Popular biographies and histories treating the era of the Revolution and the Founding Fathers were published in growing numbers, a process capped by the monumental volumes of Bancroft which began appearing in the mid-thirties.

Yet there was something specious in this historicism of the Americans. As a mobile people with a loose attachment to place and impermanent institutions, many persons felt compelled to demonstrate their loyalties and faith in past ideals. But history served as glorious example, seldom as binding precedent. The self-conscious identity celebrated on the Fourth and other occasions provided a sense of unity and place in an otherwise rootless and shifting environment. At the same time Americans seldom conceived of themselves as tied to historical time in the strictest sense, since this would have meant that they would be part of the cycles of history which, in their minds, had corrupted the Old World. To affirm their belief in progress, therefore, Americans often insisted on their newness. Their nation, they contended, was unique and uncorrupted; their limitless lands and republican institutions would keep it so. "American glory," proclaimed Noah Webster in 1825, "begins at the dawn." "Our national birth," stated a writer for the *Democratic Review* in 1839, "was the beginning of a new history . . . which separates us from the past and connects us with the future only."

In everyday life the ordinary citizen, through believing in a romanticized version of his nation's past, was not encumbered by a strong sense of historic tradition. Tocqueville noted this, stating that "among democratic nations new families are constantly springing up, others are constantly falling away, and all that remain change their condition; the woof of time is every instant broken and the track of generations effaced. Those who went before are soon forgotten; of those who come after, no one has any

idea: the interest of man is confined to those in close pro-
pinquity to himself." Cooper's Bragg expressed similar sentiments: "Why, sir," he declared to an English gentleman,
"in the way of history, one meets with but few encum-
brances in this country, but he may do very much as interest dictates, so far as that is concerned, at least. A nation
is much to be pitied that is weighed down by the past, in
this manner, since its industry and enterprise are constantly impeded by obstacles that grow out of its recollections."

Americans could more easily view themselves as being
immune to the influences of historical time by being ex-
pansionists. The idea of the West and its settlement as a
continual renewal was a strong one, going back to the
period of Franklin and Jefferson. The sense of American
boundlessness was captured in a folk tale about a legendary
Kentuckian who, when asked the boundaries of the United
States, explained: "Why sir, on the north we are bounded
by the Aurora Borealis, on the east we are bounded by the
rising sun, on the south we are bounded by the procession
of the Equinoxes, and on the west by the Day of Judgment." In 1839 the Whig Caleb Cushing spoke explicitly
of expansionism as a means of postponing the historical
cycle. "I consider it," he stated, "the destiny of the United
States to people, cultivate, and civilize this Continent; and
I anticipate no end of her power until the appointed work
be done." In other words, until the United States completed
its divine mission of expansion, its star would remain in the
ascendancy.

But while expansionism provided a psychological safety
valve that allowed persons to believe that America had, at
least for the present, escaped historic time and collapse, it
created other tensions of its own. For one thing, the rapid
settlement of the West during the first half of the nineteenth century weakened such earlier institutions of social

control as the family, church, bench and bar, landholding and merchant elites, and the state. Many persons, of course, welcomed these changes as the fruition of democratic individualism—the triumph of the self-reliant common man. Emersonian transcendentalism epitomized this faith in a society of free individuals operating without institutional restraints. But for others the image of such an unchecked individualism conjured up fears of anarchy and immorality.

The initial reaction of eastern conservatives fearful of the West was one of contempt. Typical of this attitude was Yale President Timothy Dwight's description of frontier settlers as "too idle; too talkative; too passionate; too prodigal; and too shiftless; to acquire either property or character." Dwight went on to lament the frontiersman's impatience with "the restraints of law, religion, and morality," and their unwillingness to pay taxes "by which Rulers, Ministers, and School-masters, are supported."

Gradually, however, orthodox Easterners developed the notion that the West could be kept under control through an expanding evangelical Protestantism. An educated ministry was needed for the West, noted a writer for the *Quarterly Journal of the American Education Society* in 1828, "to dispel ignorance, check vice, and create a pure public opinion, favorable to sound morals and true religion." The society publishing this journal had been organized in 1815 in Boston in order to subsidize the college and seminary training of future ministers. Other interdenominational Protestant societies that were established between 1815 and 1826 for similar purposes included the American Home Missionary Society of New York, which paid the expenses of many pastors traveling west, and even the salaries of some with poor congregations; the American Bible Society and the American Tract Society, which distributed millions of Bibles and moral pamphlets respectively between the 1820's and the Civil War; and the

American Sunday School Union. Both clergy and laity supported these societies, though, as Charles S. Griffin has shown, the leadership was largely composed of influential laymen.

Typical of these leaders was Theodore Frelinghuysen. A devout Presbyterian, Whig politician and senator from New Jersey from 1829 to 1835, Clay's running mate in the unsuccessful Whig campaign of 1844, and President of Rutgers, Frelinghuysen at various periods from 1829 to 1862 had also served as vice-president of the Education and Home Missionary societies and the Sunday School Union, and as president of the Bible and the Tract societies. In all of these positions he attempted to promote an orderly God-fearing America governed by the Gospel and sound (i.e. conservative) political principles. Speaking of the West before the Sunday School Union in 1830, Frelinghuysen warned that new settlers, "but yesterday born into political existence," would if unchecked exhibit a "universal degeneracy of manners." Violence and general disobedience of the law could only be curbed by the "reformation of the public sentiment" through religion.

The urgency of evangelizing the West was pressed not merely because of the supposed degeneracy there, but, more significantly, because it was believed that political power was moving westward. By converting the men of the West, it was hoped that both the moral and the political order of the nation would be preserved. "Before the present generation shall have passed off the stage," prophesized a writer for the Education Society in 1828, "the 'star of empire' will have taken 'its way westward,' and the consequence will be either a blessing or a curse just in the degree that virtuous or vicious principles prevail among the people." Without the spread of revivals in the West, declared a writer for the Home Missionary Society in 1845, "the state will be the synonym of anarchy—Law the refuge and charter of violence—Justice the incarnation of partiality and revenge. The stations of power will be the prizes of an ambition instinct with outrage and crime."

In 1832 the fifty-seven-year-old Reverend Lyman Beecher left his Boston ministry to head the newly formed Lane Theological Seminary at Cincinnati. Beecher, a somber man who looked upon seventeenth-century Puritan New England as the "most perfect society," had watched with growing apprehension the transformation of America from the days of the Revolution through the 1820's. During this time he had become one of the staunchest advocates of a modified evangelical Calvinism, preaching a millennial vision of the reign of Christ in a community of propriety, order, and temperance. He saw the role of revivalist religion as saving the world from papal despotism and the nation from sin and anarchy. Though not antiprogressive, for him the progress of the Republic was dependent on religion. "Give up the Sabbath," he thundered, "and the reign of chaos . . . will return." "Thus endeth the nation that despised the Lord." In the words of a recent student, Barbara M. Cross, Beecher's appeal was to "the people of small farms . . . who gloried in the looming greatness of America but longed to shape it in their own image. If they welcomed territorial expansion, they were nervous as they watched their children go to the city or the West and were suspicious of the strange ways of the city merchant, the Southern plantation owner, the society belle, the Catholic immigrant. Beecher addressed himself to a worried people, who found relief in the violent and simple lucidity of his counsel."

Revivalists like Beecher aimed primarily at reforming the individual. Once enough persons accepted Christ, it was assumed that society would be on the path toward its sober millennium. In their stress on the individual, these conservative clergymen shared much in common with the radical

reformers of the age. Others, however, though equally ap-
prehensive about America, argued that reform must begin
with institutional change, not individual redemption.

An exemplar of this position was Horace Bushnell, a
Congregational minister of Hartford and one of the country's outstanding theologians. Liberal in his theology, rejecting the idea of total depravity and insisting on freedom
of the will, Bushnell was, nevertheless, highly conservative
in his social and economic views. He was particularly concerned with bolstering the institutional basis of Christianity in the age of disestablishment. In his book, *Christian
Nurture* (1847), he attacked the revivalist emphasis for its
reliance on individual conversion, and stressed instead a
total Christian environment in which children would be
raised as members of the family, the church, and the community. In such an institutionalized environment, he rea-
soned, Christianity would be a total and lifelong commitment, not a single experience. Yet even Bushnell admitted
that revivalist preachers were "admirably adapted . . . to
the new west—a kind of light artillery that God has organized to pursue and overtake the fugitives that flee into
the wilderness from his presence . . . . The new settler
reaches the ground to be occupied, and, by the next week,
he is likely to find the circuit crossing by his door and to
hear the voice of one crying in the wilderness, 'The kingdom
of God is come nigh unto you.'"

Besides revivals and renewed emphasis on Christian environment, another means by which persons tried to
achieve social control in the flux of Jacksonian America was
through reform, particularly the temperance movement
and the extension of education. In a recent sociological
study Joseph R. Gusfield argues that the organized temperance movement as it emerged nationally around the
time of Jackson's first administration represented "the
reaction of the old Federalist aristocracy to the loss of

political, social, and religious dominance in American society." Significantly, one of the major leaders of the American Temperance Society (founded in 1826), was Lyman Beecher. His *Six Sermons on Temperance* (1826), one of the major documents of the movement, attacked intemperance as undermining both church and state. "When the laboring classes are contaminated," wrote Beecher, "the right of suffrage becomes the engine of destruction . . . . As intemperance increases, the power of taxation will come more and more into the hands of men of intemperate habits and desperate fortunes; of course the laws will gradually become subservient to the debtor and less efficacious in protecting the rights of property."

Others saw the extension of education as the most effective means of preserving social control and ending society's ailments. Since the founding of the republic, numerous advocates of increased education had stressed it as a necessity for the success of republicanism. But by the 1830's a new emphasis on the need for educational reform as a means of checking unrest among the lower classes was frequently heard. Horace Mann termed education the best method of turning the common man away from the "wanton destruction of the property of others." Edward Everett in appealing to wealthy Boston businessmen for funds to support a newly established college in Ohio stated: "They ask you to contribute, to give security to your property by diffusing the means of light and truth."

Doubts about America's future in the 1820's and 1830's were not limited to conservative, orthodox New Englanders of Federalist background. As Marvin Meyers has shown, fears that expansion and industrialization were sullying the ideals of the old Republic were central to what he terms *The Jacksonian Persuasion.* According to Meyers, the Jacksonian appeal drew its strength from anxieties—"the grinding uncertainties, the shocking changes, the complexity and indirection of the new economic ways." By attacking the Bank, special privilege, paper money, and the new speculative oligarchy, these Jacksonians hoped to "re-establish continuity with that golden age in which liberty and progress were joined inseparably with simple yeoman virtues."

That such sentiments were frequently expressed both overtly and covertly by supporters of Old Hickory is undeniable. But one could build a strong case to the effect that these moral fears were shared by many Whigs as well. The Whig journal, *The American Review,* for example, in an 1845 article on "The Influence of the Trading Spirit on the Social and Moral Life in America" warned that the restless material ambition in the country was "far from being a desirable restlessness or natural condition." Such acquisitiveness was "destructive to the happiness, and dangerous to the virtue of the generation exposed to it." Even farming regions were said to be "infected with the same anxious spirit of gain." Similarly Horace Mann, who was a Whig politician as well as an educational reformer, noted gloomily "how the excitements which our institutions supply have wrought upon the love of gain and the love of place . . . . Wherever there is a signal of gain, or of power, the vultures of cupidity and of ambition darken the air. Young men launch into this tumultuous life, years earlier than has ever been witnessed elsewhere. They seek to win those prizes without delay, which, according to Nature's ordinances and appointments, are the rewards of a life of labor."

Not just Jacksonians, Whigs, and old-line Federalists, but Americans generally appeared at times uneasy about the present and future while looking longingly backwards to a supposed golden age. This was reflected in the nostalgic and sentimental tone of much popular culture. Ladies' magazines, gift books, and annuals that graced the tables in parlors of the middle classes presented a highly romantic image of the American as tender, tearful, maudlin, moral, and high-minded. Stories invariably presented heroes and heroines of pristine purity, luxuriating in a pastoral setting surrounded by untarnished nature.

The popularity of the plantation novel, in the North as well as the South, from the mid-1820's to the Civil War evinced, as William R. Taylor has pointed out, the need many Americans felt to believe in the existence of a landed, aristocratic, static, and nonpecuniary society. Such a chivalric image, while flattering the South and serving in the defense of slavery, was nearly as important in easing a northern conscience made guilty by an unsettling materialism. As Taylor writes, persons "sought to counterpoint the limitations of the Yankee ethos by summoning before their Northern contemporaries the legendary Southern gentleman, who seemed to possess every quality which the Yankee lacked: honor and integrity, indifference to money and business, a decorous concern for the amenities, and a high sense of civic and social responsibility."

Popular music of the Jacksonian era was similarly sentimental, nostalgic, and antimaterialistic. In a ballad commemorating the completion of the Erie Canal in 1825, Samuel Woodworth (a popular poet, playwright, and journalist) specifically stressed the nonmonetary significance of the canal:

> *Yet, it is not that Wealth now enriches the*
> * scene,*
> *Where the treasures of Art and of Nature,*
> * convene;*
> *'Tis not that this union [of waters] our*
> * coffers may fill—*
> *O! no—it is something more exquisite still.*

> *'Tis, that Genius has triumph'd—and Science*
>   *prevail'd,*
> *Tho' Prejudice flouted, and Envy assail'd,*
> *It is, that the vassals of Europe, may see*
> *The progress of mind, in a land that is free.*

The retrospective mood of the age combined with a reverence for family, nature, and place was captured in a popular song by George P. Morris, "Woodman, Spare that Tree" (1837):

> *Woodman, spare that tree!*
> *Touch not a single bough;*
> *In youth it sheltered me,*
> *And I'll protect it now;*
> *'Twas my forefather's hand,*
> *That placed it near his cot,*
> *There woodman let it stand,*
> *Thy axe shall harm it not!*

Other songs which became sentimental standbys in bustling mid-nineteenth-century America were such favorites as John Howard Payne's "Home Sweet Home" (1823), with its wistful depiction of old-fashioned family life, and Samuel Woodworth's "The Old Oaken Bucket" (1825), with its evocations of a simple rural past. The height of popular musical pathos of this sort was reached in the songs of Stephen Foster. Such softhearted and mournful ditties as "Old Folks at Home" (1851), "My Old Kentucky Home" (1853), and "Jeanie with the Light Brown Hair" (1854), played on the guilt Americans felt due to their lack of unchanging old family homesteads where one lived simply and peacefully from birth to death.

Regret for the forsaken home even found its way into political rhetoric. Henry Clay, usually thought of as the spokesman for a forward-looking and mobile people, in an

1832 speech played on the parochial pieties of migrant Americans. He described the despair of the western settler "separated, forever, from the roof under which the companions of his childhood were sheltered, from the trees which have shaded him from summer's heats, the spring from whose gushing fountain he has drunk in his youth, the tombs that hold the precious relics of his venerated ancestors!"

As steam and factory changed the face of America, people became particularly tender in talking of childhood, motherhood, the family, and the home. Women and children were increasingly revered as embodiments of naturalness, innocence, and morality. A man's world was depicted as hurried and sordid—tainted by materialism and the ethics of competitive cupidity, whereas women and children were free spirits safe in the moral sanctuary of the home. That many women were being forced by economic necessity into industrial employment while others were luxuriating in the world of high fashion did not escape observant Americans and only added to the discords and tensions of the age. So too did the earlier Calvinist concept of the evil nature of children clash with the newer philosophy of the natural virtue and simple innocence of the child. But these conflicts and contradictions tended to be glossed over or completely ignored in favor of assuring, moralistic meliorisms.

On occasions, however, the darker bodings that many persons felt were expressed in grim prophecies of doom and decay. That the prosperous appearance of society could be disrupted by a volcano-like cataclysm was not an uncommon thought. The Millerites waiting on hilltops for the end of the world in 1843 and 1844 were not unique. The Reverend Ephram Peabody warned in 1846: "All may be smooth and fair on the surface, the sides of the mountain may be covered with verdure, the shepherd may keep his flocks, and the vineyards may put forth leaves, and the clusters may ripen in the sun, but the fires of a volcano are moving beneath the thin crust, and without warning, in a moment, they may burst through, and lay the labors of centuries in ruins." Nine years later, the Reverend Richard Storrs catalogued the dangers confronting America—infidelity, vice, crime, slavery, and a growing number of Catholics swarming "like locusts in the land." "If, even now," he continued, "we be not sleeping on the crater's edge, whose fiery floods threaten an overflow of our civil and religious liberties more terrible than was felt by Pompeii or Herculaneum, the signs of the times and the interpretations of prophecy deceive us!"

The vision of a cataclysmic event terminating the peaceful process of historic development was a common one. A list of novels, poems, paintings, and historical works produced between the War of 1812 and the Civil War on the theme of annihilation could be extended almost without limit. Popular paintings depicting destruction included Ashur Durand's *God's Judgement upon Gog,* Thomas Cole's *Expulsion from Paradise* and *Destruction* from his *The Course of Empire* series, Rembrandt Peale's *The Court of Death,* Benjamin West's *Death on a Pale Horse,* and Joshua Shaw's *The Deluge* (plate 2). Irving's *Conquest of Granada* (1842), William Prescott's *Conquest of Mexico* (1843) and *Conquest of Peru* (1847), and William Gilmore Simms' 1832 story of the sinking of the island of Atlantis were examples of what a recent literary historian has called the "American School of Catastrophe." In 1830 the Reverend Thomas Gray wrote a novel, *The Vestal,* that dwelled on the destruction of Pompeii; seven years later William Ware's *Letters from Palmyra,* dealing with the fall of Roman civilization, became a best seller. In his long poem "The Deluge" (1839) Rufus Dawes described a comet approaching the earth and causing the oceans to rise; at the crest of the flood the fires of the earth's center burst out

2.   Joshua Shaw, *The Deluge*

in flaming lava: "Beasts and birds/ Forests, and towers, and palaces together/ Rushed to promiscuous ruin . . . ."

Two of the most morbid, melancholy, and popular of the many catastrophists were the now-forgotten Davidson sisters. Lucretia, the elder, began her literary career at the age of nine in 1817, with an ode on a dead robin. By thirteen she was luridly describing the drowning of the Egyptian hosts in the Red Sea in her "Exit from Egyptian Bondage." In 1822 she mused morbidly on the "Destruction of Sodom and Gomorrah" and the "Ruin of Palmyra." She was in the process of writing of the "dread of madness" that "sweeps on wild destruction's wing" when she died in 1825, at the age seventeen.

Margaret, her equally gloomy younger sister (b. 1823,

d. 1838), began her morose career at the age of eleven with a poem "Belshazzar's Feast" detailing the doom of a once mighty kingdom. Following her sister's earlier example, Margaret also wrote on "The Destruction of Sodom and Gomorrah." The Lord's obliteration of these cities was told with calamitous vividness. In their day, the poetry of these child celebrants of catastrophe was taken seriously, as witnessed by the fact that Samuel F. B. Morse and Washington Irving wrote lives of Lucretia and Margaret respectively. Even the Poet Laureate of England, Robert Southey, reviewed Lucretia's poems in the British *Quarterly Review.*

The large body of catastrophic art and literature make it clear that the pervasive pessimism of Hawthorne and Melville, and the macabre melancholy of Poe were not out of touch with the age, but were sensitive responses to America's anxieties. These great writers went beyond the didactic horror of their contemporaries and were able to use the holocaust genre to convey tragic irony, thematic allegory, and psychological terror. They knew, as others only sensed, that progressive America was not immune to the ravages of time. As the young Melville wrote in *Mardi* (1848), "though crimson republics may rise in constellations, like fiery Aldebarans, speeding to their culminations; yet, down must they sink at last, and leave the old sultan-sun in the sky; in time, again to be deposed."

CHAPTER THREE

The Industrial Road to "The Celestial City"

T HE WEALTHY BOSTON ASSOCIATES WHO CONTROLLED northern New England's expanding cotton industry were not pleased with the politics of President Jackson. Kirk Boott, the powerful manager of the corporation's factories at Lowell, campaigning for Clay in 1832, declared: "Elect General Jackson and the grass will grow in your streets, owls will build their nests in the mills, and foxes burrow in your highways." Yet less than a year later, when it was learned that the touring President intended to visit Lowell, the corporation directors, aware of the publicity value of such an appearance, overcame their political scruples long enough to make the affair a gala occasion. No expenses were spared: "We will feed him on gold dust, if he will eat it," stated Amos Lawrence, one of the richest of the Boston elite.

Thousands of persons crowded into Lowell on the morning of June 27, 1833, to witness the parade and catch a glimpse of the President. The weather, which had been threatening, conveniently cleared in the late morning, and, just after noon, loud shouts spread the news of Jackson's arrival. Riding in an open barouche, accompanied by Martin Van Buren and several of Lowell's leading stockholders, Jackson passed between two hickory trees specially transplanted for the occasion and beneath banners commemorating his victory at New Orleans and his strong stand against nullification. After some welcoming speeches, the guest of honor was led to the balcony of the town's best hotel to witness the parade.

Ill-trained militia men, town selectmen, police and firemen, and the school committee led the procession. But the most striking feature of the parade consisted of 2,500 girls dressed in white muslin with blue sashes, carrying blue or green parasols. These girls were factory operatives—part of a new type of labor force which was already world renowned. Marching two abreast, their line stretched for more than a mile, making an impressive sight. "Very pretty women, by the Eternal!" proclaimed the old General, bowing from his balcony as each couple came by. Following the procession, the President was led into one of the mills where some of the prettiest of the girls, still in their festive costumes, were tending the machines. The picture was one of pleasant, progressive labor—the very opposite of the traditional American image of industrial employment. When Jackson left Lowell, it was with a more positive attitude toward manufactures.

About a year later another distinguished Westerner came to witness the Lowell phenomenon. Colonel Davy Crockett was already a legendary figure when he arrived at Lowell in May of 1834. As with Jackson, Crockett was shown every respect by the astute directors. Abbott Lawrence presented the backwoodsman with a suit made from the company's fabric, which Crockett claimed was of "as good cloth as the best I ever bought as best ever imported." The kindness shown Crockett paid off in publicity dividends in 1835 when he published his widely read *Tour to the North and Down*

East. Like Jackson, he was most unstinting in his praise of the female operatives. "We stopped at a large stone house at the head of the falls of the Merrimack River," he wrote, "and having taken a little refreshment, went down among the factories. The dinner-bells were ringing and the folks pouring out of the houses like bees out of gum. I looked at them as they passed, all well-dressed, lively and genteel in their appearance, indeed the girls looked as if they were coming from a quilting frolic . . . . I went in among the young girls, and talked with many of them. Not one expressed herself as tired of her employment, or oppressed with work; all talked well, and looked healthy. Some of them were very handsome . . . ."

Continuing, Colonel Crockett explained the precise significance of Lowell: "I could not help reflecting on the differences between these females, thus employed, and those of other populous countries, where the female character is degraded to abject slavery. Here were thousands, useful to others, and enjoying all the blessings of freedom, with the prospect before them of future comfort and respectability . . . . I regret that more of our southern and western men do not go there, as it would help to do away with their prejudices against these manufactories."

Such praise for Lowell and its workers was becoming commonplace by the 1830's, but coming from Andrew Jackson and Davy Crockett, it was of particular importance. Although they disagreed politically, Crockett having broken with Jackson and joined the Whigs, both were heroic figures—American Adams and symbols of the frontier West. They stood out as leaders and representatives of an untrammelled agrarian people who lived close to nature and derived moral virtues from that closeness. That such persons could also extol the new world of factory and machine implied that these forces were not a violation of nature; that their appearance in America would neither signal the decline of republican simplicity and virtue nor usher in the poverty and degradation that Americans considered characteristic of European manufacturing.

The emergence of this image of Lowell had not been accidental. When Francis Cabot Lowell and his fellow investors first introduced the power loom into America, they were aware of existing prejudices against manufactures. In the words of Nathan Appleton, one of the original directors, it was widely known that "the operatives in the manufacturing cities of Europe were notoriously of the lowest character, for intelligence and morals. The question therefore arose, and was deeply considered, whether this degradation was the result of the peculiar occupation or of other and distinct causes." Appleton and the others set out to prove that industrial employment did not inevitably result in physical and moral deterioration. It seems clear from their letters and journals that these men conceived of their task as a moral one. They hoped to free America from dependence on European manufactures and yet accomplish this without corrupting an Edenic society. In this regard they shared the same sense of divine mission as the agrarian idealists. "Ours is a great novel experiment," proclaimed Appleton. "Whatever the result, it is our destiny to make it. It is our mission—our care should be to understand it and make it succeed."

Yet if these men were to establish an industrial utopia, they realized some new source of labor must be found. Where manufacturing had developed in the early nineteenth century, there appeared every indication that American factories would follow in the same exploitive path as European industries. The first factories of any significance in this country were the spinning mills of southern New England, almost all of which were modeled on Samuel Slater's original Pawtucket plant. By the War of 1812, there were several hundred small mills turning raw cotton into yarn. The employers generally owned the town as well as the mill, and a type of neofeudalism developed. Whole families were hired; those with a large number of children were preferred, since the mills depended mostly on child labor. Wages were low and frequently paid in the form of credits at the company's store. Poverty and exploitation were the rule, and few workingmen came out financially ahead.

While such a system had sufficed for these small spinning mills, clearly it was not a satisfactory model for the large-scale factories planned by the Boston Associates. It was doubtful if enough employees could be induced to accept such a system, and public reaction would have been strongly negative. Therefore, rather than hiring whole families and relying heavily on child labor, the Boston industrialists hit upon the idea of employing unmarried New England farm girls in their late teens and early twenties.

This plan had much to recommend it. For one thing, New England farming had long been in a state of decline, and the labor of numerous females was not in great demand. Then too there was a common notion that young women who were not regularly occupied would be led into vicious habits. Industrial employment, it was argued, would serve to keep these "useless" girls from idleness, thereby turning a financial burden into an asset, and relieving society of a potentially immoral class. An added advantage in the eyes of the manufacturers was the fact that these farmers' daughters had been brought up to expect hard work, little pay, and long hours. Furthermore, most were educated and could readily be taught machine skills.

In order to quell fears that a factory environment would corrupt the rural girls, the Boston Associates devised an elaborate system of paternalistic supervision. Unless living with approved relations, the operatives were required to take their room and board in company-owned boarding houses under the watchful eye of respectable women. Provisions were made for religious worship, which was required, and for educational activities. A ten o'clock curfew was rigidly enforced and any unseemly conduct was considered grounds for immediate dismissal. "Under these circumstances," in Appleton's words, "the daughters of respectable farmers were readily induced to come into these mills for a temporary period."

First tried at Waltham during the War of 1812 and more extensively used with the opening of Lowell in 1823, this system seemed successful in every way. The heavily mechanized and financed factories easily withstood British competition while returning dividends that averaged close to twenty per cent annually and in some years as much as forty per cent. Success led to expansion, and within a generation the Boston Associates had major mills in operation throughout southern Maine and New Hampshire and northern Massachusetts. But perhaps the greatest triumph of the Boston investors was in creating a progressive industrial image acceptable to agrarian America. In this regard Lowell was their showplace; it soon became the most significant symbol of New World industrialism.

Only four years after Lowell's inception, the noted British traveler Captain Basil Hall made a point of visiting these mills. Struck by the vivid contrast between Lowell and English factory towns, Hall in his popular *Travels in North America,* portrayed this New World manufactory in glowing terms. "The whole discipline, ventilation, and other arrangements," he wrote, "appeared to be excellent, of which the best proof was the healthy and cheerful look of the girls, all of whom, by the way, were trigged out with much neatness and simplicity, and wore high tortoise-shell combs at the back of their heads." Awakened at six in the morning by the tolling of the factory bells, Hall, "on looking from the window, saw the whole space between the factories and the village speckled over with girls, nicely dressed, and glittering with bright shawls and showy-colored gowns and gay bonnets, all streaming along to their business, with an air of lightness, and elasticity of step, implying an obvious desire to get to their work."

Between Hall's 1827 visit and the Civil War, virtually all of the many foreign observers in America went to admire Lowell. It became as important on the traveler's itinerary as Niagara Falls, Washington, a slave auction, a prison, or an Indian encampment. Invariably Lowell was described as "clean," "fresh," "new," "moral," "healthy." To the Frenchman Michel Chevalier, a student of industrialism, Lowell in 1834 was "neat, orderly, quiet, and prudent," unlike any industrial center he had ever seen. Harriet Martineau, the curious, sympathetic, ear-trumpted English tourist, visiting Lowell that same year, noted approvingly the "neat," "spacious" town with its churches, lyceum, library, and "well-dressed young ladies." When Charles Dickens went there in 1842, Lowell was nearly two decades old; yet it was the quality of newness that most impressed him: "The very river that moves the machinery in the mills . . . seems to acquire a new character from the fresh buildings of bright red brick and painted wood among which it takes its course; and to be as light-headed, thoughtless, and brisk a young river, in its murmurings and tumblings, as one would desire to see. One would swear that every 'Bakery,' 'Grocery,' and 'Bookbindery,' and other kind of store, took its shutters down for the first time, and started in business yesterday. The golden pestles and mortars fixed as signs upon the sun-blind frames outside the Druggists', appear to have been just turned out of the United States' Mint; and when I saw a baby of some ten days old in a woman's arms at a street corner, I found myself unconsciously wondering where it came from: never supposing for an instant that it could have been born in such a young town as that."

Dickens was at Lowell during the brief period (1840–45), when the female operatives published their own literary magazine, *The Lowell Offering*. He warned his English readers that they might be startled to learn of the existence of such a publication, but that despite the fact that it was "written by these girls after the arduous labours of the day, . . . it will compare advantageously with a great many English Annuals. It is pleasant to find that many of its Tales are of the Mills and of those who work in them; that they inculcate habits of self-denial and contentment, and teach good doctrines of enlarged benevolence. A strong feeling for the beauties of nature, as displayed in the solitudes the writers have left at home, breathes through its pages like wholesome village air. . . ."

The Lowell workers themselves seldom viewed their toil in the same light as did the visiting dignitaries. As shall be related in the next chapter, the actual working conditions were anything but utopian. But at least a few of the Lowell girls did have a sense of participating in a novel experiment that presaged great things for America's future. One of the most articulate of the early laborers who has left an account of those years was Lucy Larcom, later well-known as a poetess. Miss Larcom had come to Lowell as a small child with her widowed mother who had taken a job as a keeper of one of the company boarding houses. Because of her mother's financial difficulties, Lucy went to work in the mills before she was twelve, though child labor of this sort was not usual. Her working hours were long, running from sunrise to sunset, but her work was easy, consisting of changing bobbins on the spinning-frames. She remembered having much free time which she and the other young girls "spent frolicking around among the spinning-frames, teasing and talking to the older girls, or entertaining ourselves with games and stories in a corner, or exploring with the overseer's permission, the mysteries of the carding-room, the dressing-room, and the weaving-room." To her, the mill "was far from being a disagreeable place to stay in. The girls were bright-looking and neat, and everything was kept clean and shiny. The effect of the whole was rather attractive to strangers."

One facet of early Lowell that Miss Larcom particularly praised in her reminiscence was its rural appearance. "Nature," she remembered, "came very close to the mill-gates . . . . There was green grass all around them; violets and wild geraniums grew by the canals; and long stretches of open land between the corporation buildings and the streets made the town seem country-like." Outside observers also noted this. Fredrika Bremer, the Swedish novelist, described Lowell's setting as "beautiful." "The views from the higher parts of the town, as far as the White Mountains of New Hampshire which raise their snowy crowns above every other object, are extensive and magnificent." An English clergyman visiting Lowell in the mid-1840's wrote that in the bright sunshine the "fresh and flourishing" trees and neat gardens gave to this "city of factories" a distinctly rural appearance.

In part, the rural look of Lowell and other early factory towns resulted from the fact that water power rather than steam was utilized. As a New Hampshire mill owner wrote in the early 1830's: "In this country *water-power* is almost exclusively used in manufactures, and, on account of its greater cheapness, the day must be far distant indeed, when steam power will be extensively used; the consequence is, that the manufacturing population must be scattered. We have no Manchesters on this side of the Atlantic, while our thousand rivers and streams afford an inexhaustible supply of unimproved power."

But this ruralness also stemmed from a conscious effort

on the part of the manufacturers to avoid the evils of European industrialism. To many Americans the degradation of the Old World industrial worker was more the result of urban conditions than of industry itself. Patrick Tracy Jackson, one of Lowell's originators, reporting for a group of northern manufacturers in 1832, stated: "In Europe, manufactures are established in large cities, the business is followed from parent to child, and wages are so miserably low, that few families can be supported without parochial aid. One consequence of this abject poverty is, that children are set to work at a very tender age, and have no time allowed for education, literary or moral. In the United States, manufactories are dispersed through the country."

The spot chosen for the building of Lowell, on the Merrimack River just above its junction with the Concord, was a place of great natural beauty with gently rolling hills on either side of the rapid river. Kirk Boott, who planned the location and design of the mills and boarding houses, took advantage of the setting. As John Coolidge points out in an excellent book on Lowell architecture, the original mills had a simple dignified appearance that was enhanced by the open spaces between them where the stream could be viewed. The boarding houses, some of wood, some of brick, were separated from one another by a strip of lawn; broad grass areas planted with trees and shrubs also set the factories apart from the houses. The whole effect was peaceful and inviting.

The rural character of Lowell and other factory towns made it easier for individuals to reconcile the myth of America as a new Eden with the sudden appearance of the machine. It allowed persons to hold to the Jeffersonian concept of the moral virtues of country life, while simultaneously participating in industrialization. Material advance through technology, in other words, would not sacrifice morality. This notion was implicit in much of the pro-industrial writing of the period. A northern New England factory manager, for instance, reported in the mid-thirties that "nearly all of the manufacturing villages are small, and there is very generally attached to each dwelling a lot of ground, which is appropriated to the culture of garden vegetables, and food for a cow and swine; these are considered very essential comforts, and are rarely dispensed with by the industrious operatives." Similarly Harriet Martineau noted: "It always gave me pleasure to see the artisans at work about such places as Glen's Falls, the Falls of the Genesee, and on the banks of some of the whirling streams in the New England valleys. I felt that they caught, or might catch, as beautiful glimpses of Nature's face as the western settler." In America, she concluded, there was little distinction between "the agency of vegetation or of steam," for both sustained man morally and materially.

Not only was it argued by the advocates of manufacturing that such endeavors were ethical, but they also claimed that increased industrialization would stimulate agriculturalists to become more moral and more productive themselves. This line of reasoning was expressed by virtually every defender of manufacturing from Hamilton and Tench Coxe to the political spokesman of the Boston Associates, Daniel Webster. One of the most thoughtful proponents of this position, Daniel Raymond, wrote in his *Thoughts on Political Economy* (1820) that "among a people whose wants are confined to the necessaries of life, as is almost entirely the case with all savage nations, it is notorious that agriculture is never carried to any degree of perfection. Our industry is always in proportion to our wants, or to our motives to labour; and where his wants are confined to the mere necessaries of life, man is an indolent, slothful animal. But the case is entirely changed when the comforts and luxuries of life come to constitute a portion of his wants . . . . Manufactures come to have a value; manufacturing labour becomes productive; its product stimulates the agriculturalist to greater exertion; a re-action is produced; the wilderness is converted into a fruitful field; and savage man into the polished enlightened citizen." This is an interesting argument since it depicts the increased acquisitiveness created by industrialization as a moralizing force, helping to turn "savage" "wilderness" into "enlightened," "fruitful field." The true Garden, in other words, could only be created through manufacturing.

Writing in the mid-1830's, George White, Slater's laudatory biographer, expressed a somewhat analogous argument. "A nation peopled only by farmers," he wrote, "must be a region of indolence and misery. If the soil is naturally fertile, little labour will produce abundance; but for want of exercise even that little labour will be burdensome and often neglected. Want will be felt in the midst of abundance . . . . Those therefore who wish to make agriculture flourish in any country, can have no hope of succeeding in the attempt but by bringing commerce and manufactures to her aid; which by taking from the farmer his superfluous produce, gives spirit to his operations, and life and activity to his mind."

This combination of industrial logic and romanticism, together with a rising economic nationalism which swept America after 1815, won for the New England textile manufacturers and other industrial advocates a large measure of public support and worldwide fame. Industrial production grew rapidly. By 1835 an observant American noted that "manufacturing, instead of going on quietly and single-handed in private families, with immense labour, grows into large establishments, which employ and bring into association, masses of the population." Two years later, Francis Grund clearly perceived the enthusiasm with which Americans accepted manufacturing. "Town and country," he wrote, "rival with each other in the eagerness of industrial pursuits. Machines are invented, new lines of communication established, and the depths of the sea explored to afford scope for the spirit of enterprise; and it is as if all America were but one gigantic workshop, over the entrance of which there is the blazing inscription *'No admission here except on business.'* "

"The manufactures of the United States," continued Grund, "have kept equal pace with the extension of commerce. The states of Massachusetts, Pennsylvania, New York, and New Jersey have taken the lead; but the same spirit of enterprise is manifesting itself in every quarter of the union. America possesses all the requisites of a manufacturing country, water, coal, and a highly ingenious, inventive population . . . . There is scarcely an article which does not furnish them with new means of exercising their ingenuity. Thus a large trade is carried on, by the people of New England, in painted chairs, which are sent by the thousands all over the United States, and also exported to South America, and the West Indies. The shoe trade of some of the towns in the neighborhood of Boston is hardly less remarkable, the value of nearly two millions of dollars having been manufactured last year and sent to the west alone. The state of Connecticut possesses the most extensive wooden clock manufactories in the world; affording them at about half the price of those made in the Black Forest."

The physical expansion of Jacksonian America, together with the dominant agrarian mythology, made it possible for some contemporaries (as well as many later historians) to overlook the extent of industrial growth and consolidation. Yet astute observers, then and now, understood the dual thrust of the economy which was making society more closely knit, interdependent, and productive, while at the same time expanding outward. One of the keenest witnesses of this phenomenon was Michel Chevalier who spent two years in the United States (1833–35) on a mission for the French government to study technological improvements, particularly in transportation. Chevalier distinctly saw that American society was being transformed by the machine power that was applied to transportation and industry. The country's "most suitable emblem," he believed, "would be a locomotive engine or a steamboat." His careful study of internal improvements led him to the conclusion that: "The spectacle of a young people, executing in the short space of fifteen years a series of works which the most powerful States of Europe with a population three or four times as great would have shrunk from undertaking, is in truth a noble sight. The advantages to the public prosperity which result from these enterprises are incalculable . . . ."

Statistical and demographical evidence of the changing effects technology was having on American society appeared in 1843 with the publication of George Tucker's *Progress of the United States in Population and Wealth in Fifty Years, as Exhibited by the Decennial Census from 1790 to 1840*. Tucker, in most respects a staunch Jeffersonian and holder of the first chair in Moral Philosophy at Jefferson's University of Virginia, was also an advocate of industrialization and an indefatigable investigator of this subject. Though his statistical calculations based on the census reports are rather crude by present-day standards, they do give a good indication of the actual changes occurring at the time. Among other things, Tucker concluded that wealth was growing faster than population; that industrial employment was increasing at a greater rate than any other occupation; and "that the increase of population in towns over 10,000 exceeded that of the whole population in the ratio of 50 to 32." Speaking specifically of the growth of industrial employment, he wrote: "This increase was greatest in the New En-

gland States, whose manufacturing population had enlarged from 21 per cent, in 1820, to 30.2 per cent in 1840;
in which time the same class of population had nearly
trebled in Massachusetts, and more than trebled in
Rhode Island. In the Southwestern States, alone, the
proportion of the agricultural class had increased; in all
the others it had diminished."

Economic historians for more than two decades have
debated the question of precisely when the relatively static
economy of the early years of the nineteenth century began
to grow at a more rapid and sustained rate. Though few,
if any, current scholars hold to the once traditional view
that American industrialism had its origins in the Civil
War, there remain sharp disagreements as to just when
industrialization began to have a notable impact in the
antebellum era. In 1956 W. W. Rostow argued that economic growth and the rise of per capita income were very
small prior to the 1840's, but that the economy reached
a "take-off" in the period from 1843 to 1860, beginning the
"sustained drive to maturity."

Robert E. Gallman, in a study of "Commodity Output,
1839–1899" (1960), tended to support Rostow's thesis of a
dramatic economic jump in the two decades preceding the
Civil War. Gallman, after a careful estimate of the value
added by commodity output in agriculture, mining, manufacturing, and construction for the 1839 to 1899 period,
concluded that the largest decennial increase was between
1839–59. During those years the rate of advance was fifty-
seven per cent per decade, compared with only twenty-
three per cent during the Civil War decade (1859–69), and
an average decennial increase of fifty-four per cent between
1869–99. In an influential 1961 article attacking the idea
of the Civil War as a stimulus to industrialization, Thomas
Cochran supported the findings of Rostow and Gallman,
stating that the major era of early industrialization was

from 1843 to 1857, "the first long period without a major depression, after railroads, canals, and steamboats had opened a national market . . . ."

The evidence supporting the thesis that the twenty-year period preceding the Civil War was one of rapid economic growth is very persuasive. The notion that this marked a new and dramatic "take-off," however, is highly questionable. Such a view presupposes that industrialism was insignificant prior to the 1840's. Gallman, for instance, in dating the beginnings of accelerated growth "in or before" the 1840's, expressed surprise at the high rate of increase in product per head during these "early stages of industrialization," since evidence drawn from the experience of other countries generally suggested that rapid increase comes after initial industrial growth. This surprise, of course, would be unnecessary if Gallman had taken into consideration the significant extent of industrialization prior to the 1840's.

Part of the difficulty economic historians have had in studying economic growth prior to 1840 has been the absence of reliable quantitative data before that year. Federal Census returns begin in 1790, and many states compiled decennial returns prior to 1840, but this material, according to one respected scholar, is "almost worthless." Yet, as has already been shown in this study, there exists strong contemporary evidence, impressionistic though much of it is, that industrialization was of major import as early as the 1820's and certainly in the 1830's. Recent statistical studies support this view. Douglass C. North, who has done extensive quantitative work on pre-Civil War economic growth, now dates the period of beginning acceleration from 1823 to 1843, "the years when industrialization began." He puts particular emphasis on the decade of the thirties as a period that witnessed "a radical set of changes which initiated sustained and accelerated expansion of the economy."

According to a recent book by Robert W. Fogel, one of the main reasons earlier authorities have dated the quickening of economic growth from the 1840's or later is that these scholars have assumed that an effective network of railroads was a necessary prerequisite for the industrial revolution. Fogel disagrees with this, insisting that the basic innovations in the economy preceded the railroad. He contends that the twenties correspond most closely to Rostow's description of a "take-off" era. This decade, he writes, "may have witnessed a shift toward manufacturing comparable to that observed for the 'take-off' years. This possibility is supported by the sharp decline in the home manufacture of consumer's goods and by the fact that urban population increased at twice the rate of the population as a whole. It is also buttressed by the rapid rise of the cotton textile and iron industries. The production of cotton cloth increased by over 500 per cent between 1820 and 1831 . . . . The growth of iron production outstripped that of cotton. The output of pig iron increased from 20,000 tons in 1820 to 192,000 tons in 1830, a rise of nearly 900 per cent. By 1830 iron, like textiles, was a substantial industry." Though not as spectacular as the expansion of the iron or cotton industries, Fogel also points out that the production of wool, carpets, paper, lead, sugar and molasses, salt, processed meat, steam engines, glass, shoes, and furniture all grew on the average twice to three times as fast as the population between 1820 and 1830.

If forced to choose a date for the beginnings of the rapid rise of manufactures, this author would agree with Professor Fogel in emphasizing the significance of the 1820's. The development of the factory system in textiles and other industries, the rise of the labor movement, the revolutions in canal and river transportation, the origins of the railroad system, the greater sectional economic specialization, the increased interest in technology, and other innovations of that decade gave assurance that the infant industrialism, spawned by the foreign crises and war from 1807 to 1815, would survive and prosper.

But perhaps singling out any specific period as one of "take-off" is a falsification of history. Like most major changes, the industrial revolution was a long process, not an event. What is significant is that the Jacksonian generation was involved in the technological transformation of an agrarian society into an industrial economy. To the people of the period this was a new experience. Even though this change was not completed during the pre-Civil War years, it is essential for the student of the Jacksonian era to understand that it was taking place and that contemporaries, either consciously or unconsciously, were affected by it. Many of the basic beliefs and feelings of the era were shaped to a greater or lesser degree by these economic changes.

As industry progressed and conferred material benefits on the populace, its advocates found it less and less difficult to assert its rights against the agrarian majority. Yet they continued to claim that manufacturing conferred moral benefits on mankind. Again and again, orators fastened on the image of Lowell as the model industrial utopia. In 1838 Edward Everett, one of the nation's most verbose speakers in this rhetorical age, intoned a litany to Lowell. Reminding his audience that twenty years earlier the area had comprised but "two or three poor farms," he noted that now it was "a noble city of the arts" built by "the genius of capital." He pictured "the palaces" of Lowell's industry, "her churches, . . . her school-houses, . . . the long lines of her shops and warehouses, . . . the comfortable abodes of an enterprising, industrious, and intelligent population . . . ."

Such celebrations of Lowell's virtues—and there were hundreds in the period—implied, as one spokesman stated, that "a factory entailed no degradation of character"; or as another wrote: "Manufacturing may innocently be inoculated on the agricultural system, without endangering the morals of the people." Like the revivalists who promised perfection through salvation, industrialists on occasion spoke of manufactures as the key to the millennium. "If the physical resources of the country are becoming so greatly developed," an 1845 orator advised, "the more necessity then, that those of man should be brought forward and carried to perfection."

Yet there exists strong evidence that even some of the celebrants of industry and technology were not entirely comfortable with the changes being wrought by these forces. Everett, for example, in declaiming the virtues of the industrial "arts" in the mid-thirties, could conclude that "the moral and social improvement of our race, and the possession of the skill and knowledge embodied in them, will advance, stand still, and fall together." Of course, the very notion that the "race" might "stand still" and "fall" ran completely counter to the accepted American credo. Such a statement coming from the usually ebullient Everett, in a speech aimed at lauding technology as essential to the "civilized, cultivated, moral, and religious" society, suggests that the speaker, perhaps subconsciously, entertained certain doubts about the course of technological change.

Such covert fears appear frequently in descriptions of steamboats and railroad engines. The reaction to Fulton's first western steamer described in the previous chapter was a good example. Even earlier, his *Clermont* was reported by some who saw the ship traveling at night "as a monster moving on the waters, defying the winds and tide, and breathing flames and smoke." Thirty-five years later, Dickens noted a temperance poster showing the steamboat *Alcohol* exploding, while the good ship *Temperance* sailed safely before the wind. A few years before, Chevalier had pictured a locomotive breaking into "the bosom of a vast wilderness and the midst of a profound silence" like a "flying, panting, flaming machine . . . a winged dragon vomiting forth fire and flame." Steamships and railroads, claimed a writer for *Hunt's Merchants' Magazine* in an 1840 article praising the advance of steampower in America, were "iron monsters," "dragons of mightier power, with iron muscles that never tire, breathing smoke and flame through blackened lungs, feeding upon wood and water, outrunning the race horse . . . ." Imagery such as the above, used by persons who were not, at least on the surface, ill-disposed toward machinery, reveals an unmistakable sense of anxiety and dread. There was a direct connection between the apocalyptic images described in the previous chapter and this menacing machine imagery.

Part of the fear of mechanized power was simply a realistic reaction to actual dangers. Steam engines could and did explode with alarming frequency, particularly the high-pressure type used on steamboats. Sparks from locomotives caused fires. Unguarded factory machinery not infrequently caused the loss of fingers or whole limbs.

But much of the anxiety persons felt was more subtle and psychological, stemming from the vague notion that somehow technological progress was antithetical to the romantic values of nature. If, as the late Perry Miller suggested, Americans conceived of themselves as *Nature's Nation,* then it is understandable that they should have felt a certain uneasiness about the machine. The continued references to the rural setting of the American factory helped reduce the potential conflict between the world of Nature and the world of machine.[1] But this did not elimi-

---

[1] Frequent references to the ruralness of the American factory by manufacturers and others (see pp. 75–78), also shows an uneasy, defensive attitude.

nate the tensions since, as Leo Marx and others have shown, at base a technologically oriented society presupposed an entirely different relationship of man to nature than did a nontechnological society. "The society prefigured by the myth of the Garden," wrote Marx, "would celebrate a passive accomodation to nature's law. There, survival would depend upon the organic production of growth. But, on the other hand, the machine foretold an economy designed by man's brain, and it implied an active, indeed proud, assertion of his dominion over nature."

Veneration for Nature was not just a sentimental Jeffersonian holdover in the Jacksonian era. It was central to mid-nineteenth-century culture at all levels. From the philosophic transcendentalist essays to the tenderhearted gift books and annuals, this attitude pervaded American culture. Romanticized nature dominated the novels of Cooper and Simms, the painting of the Hudson River School, the poetry of Bryant and, later, Whitman. Fiction with an urban or industrial setting was rare in the pre-Civil War period, and that which does exist generally expressed moralistic antiurban, antimachine attitudes. Consequently it was not surprising that persons felt somewhat uneasy in viewing the nation's technological progress, even when in many ways they were direct beneficiaries of this betterment.

These tensions grew more pronounced as the obvious disharmonies between workshop and wilderness became more visible. Increasingly factory towns with their clusters of workers' tenements and shops became undeniably dreary, blotting out the beauty of the American countryside. The wealthy New Yorker, Philip Hone, himself a heavy investor in industry, noticed this on an 1832 trip to Paterson, New Jersey. The town had become a "cotton spinning dirty village, which is no longer the rural retreat it formerly was. Green trees have given place to brown stone walls, and the singing of birds to the everlasting noise of spinning jennies and power looms." Pittsburgh, noted a traveler in 1833, was engulfed in clouds of smoke, giving "a gloomy cast to the beautiful hills that surround it." James Silk Buckingham a few years later reported soot everywhere in that city: clean faces were "objects of rare occurrence and clean hands still more so." The scene reminded him of "the description given in the Scriptures of the appearance of the plain of Sodom and Gomorrah, on the day after the destruction of those cities by fire, when 'the smoke of the country went up as the smoke of a furnace.'"

Even Lowell, though its glories continued to be sung by carefully guided visitors and sycophantic politicians, began to show signs of industrial squalor. From its inception there were a large number of common laborers, mostly Irish, hired to dig the canals, put up the buildings, and lay out the roads. The corporation made no housing provisions for these workers and very quickly there developed a shantytown area variously referred to as "Paddy Camp Lands," "New Dublin," or "the Acre." By the 1830's an estimated 500 persons inhabited this quarter, living mostly in overcrowded one-room cabins made of rough slab wood, turfed up to the eaves, with a window and door at one end and two small holes in the sides for air. While construction of mills and boarding houses went on almost without interruption for twenty years, there were, nevertheless, many slack seasons in which these unemployed day laborers were driven to destitution and even beggary. Lucy Larcom, who had never seen a beggar until coming to Lowell in 1835, found to her dismay that "straggling petitioners for 'cold victuals' hung around our back yard, always of Hibernian extraction . . . ."

Other aspects of Lowell also took on an increasingly drab appearance. While the corporation had planned the mill sites and boarding houses with both beauty and utility in mind, the rest of the city was allowed to develop in a haphazard manner. Not unlike a mining community, "the town," in Miss Larcom's words, "sprung up with mushroom-rapidity." Hastily built shops and stores were crowded into a small area. Many of Lowell's best lands were held off the market by the corporation, thus warping the town's natural development. With the rise in real estate values, the managers in the 1840's began utilizing more and more of the original open areas around the factories and boarding houses. No detached houses for the operatives were built after 1840, and some of those already in use were replaced by solid blocks of buildings separated only by narrow alleyways from other dwellings. Similarly, the open space along the Merrimack was closed off by new mills and extensions of older ones, until by the late forties, the once beautiful river site presented the viewer an uninterrupted visage of brick walls. By this time the idea of Lowell as a New World utopia blending forest with factory was no longer tenable. Only the continued use of water power kept it cleaner than coal-consuming Pittsburgh.

Those most sensitive to the blighting effects of industry and technology were the best artists and writers of the age. More clearly than others, they recognized the conflict of values between America's romantic and utilitarian moods. To a man they leaned toward the romantic. Thoreau's many barbs against material progress are well known. Other intellectuals expressed similar sentiments. The painter Thomas Cole, on returning to New York City from his beloved Catskills in the mid-1830's, wrote in his journal: "What is sometimes called improvement in its march makes us fear that the bright and tender flowers of the imagination shall be all crushed beneath its iron tramp . . . ." "I should like nothing better," confessed Washington Irving in 1842, "than to have plenty of money to squander on stone and mortar, and to build chateaux . . . , but I would first blow up all the cotton mills . . . and make picturesque ruins of them; and all the cotton lords should live in baronial castles . . . and the cotton spinners should be virtuous peasantry of both sexes . . . ." "Machinery is aggressive," Emerson warned a lecture audience, "all tools are in one sense edge tools, and dangerous."

Hawthorne's story, "The Celestial Railroad" (1843), captures the romantic writer's doubts about the direction in which America's material advance was leading. The story opens with a description of a typical, prosperous, go-ahead, hurried American city. It is called the City of Destruction. The residents of this booster community incorporate a railway and other improvements to facilitate an easy passage to the Celestial City. In a Kafkaesque manner, the narrator, led by one of the railroad's founders, Mr. Smooth-it-away, attempts to travel to the Celestial City. This updated *Pilgrim's Progress* ends with the narrator betrayed by his guide. He is left at the story's close riding a fiery steamboat on the river of Death.

Such allegorical darts, of course, had no effect in checking America's technological advance. They do, however, reflect an anguish that was not limited to the intellectual, though most Americans managed to make an uneasy alliance with the industrial revolution.

But while the artists and intellectuals might have been the most aware of the contrasting values industry brought to America, those most immediately and adversely affected by the economic innovations of the era were the industrial workers themselves. The following chapter will consider their changing status and conditions.

CHAPTER FOUR

"The Laboring ·Classes"

WHEN IN 1867 NAPOLEON III NAMED MICHEL Chevalier to head the Universal Exposition at Paris, the aging French minister still remembered the pleasant factory town of Lowell that he had visited some thirty-three years before. Thinking it would be of interest to Europeans to see the neat, temperate Lowell girls at work, Chevalier wrote to his old friend Charles Sumner, the distinguished senator from Massachusetts, asking if it would be possible to have some of Lowell's renowned operatives sent to Paris with their looms in order that they might perform at the exposition. To his surprise he learned that this would be impossible as there was scarcely a New England farm "girl" left at Lowell. In the intervening years between his visit and the 1860's, they had been replaced largely by Irish and French-Canadian workers. Not only was no delegation of girls from Lowell sent, but coincidentally on the very day that the Paris Exposition was formally opened, April 1, 1867, the spinners of Lowell went out on strike, demanding a reduction in their working hours.

The demise of Lowell as an industrial idyll was in itself only a minor aspect of the history of labor in the pre-Civil War years. But because Lowell had become a symbol for the virtues of American industry, its collapse as a model system was of more than passing significance.

By present-day standards, even in its earliest years, Lowell certainly would not be considered an industrial paradise. Nor for that matter did the early operatives picture it in quite the same way as those who visited. Few accounts by the farm-girl employees from the 1820's and 1830's portray Lowell as a benevolent manufacturing college where contented girls spun and wove under the kindly direction of philanthropic employers. The oft-praised paternalism of Lowell was double-edged, serving not only to uphold morality and respectability, but also to prevent any organized efforts on the part of the operatives to improve working conditions. An elaborate blacklisting system existed throughout the northern New England mills. Its purpose was to prevent either the labor organizer or the moral deviate from finding employment.

Furthermore, the Lowell arrangement was hierarchical and impersonal from the beginning. Unlike earlier American factories, the directors and officers of the company did not reside in the factory towns, but in Boston. Under them were the resident managers, superintendents, and overseers—individuals responsible only to the directors. Next in the social scale came the mechanics and operatives, with the unskilled day laborers at the bottom of the heap. Lowell's residential architecture reflected this stratification. From the Beacon Hill and Back Bay mansions of the Boston stockholders down through the Greek-columned Georgian house of Lowell's first resident executive, Kirk Boott, to the plain dormitories of the mill hands and the shacks of the Irish laborers, the housing mirrored the hierarchical social and economic structure.

When one adds to the above the extremely long hours of employment—averaging over seventy-five hours per week—at weekly wages of $1 to $2 (exclusive of room and board), one might wonder why New England farm girls were attracted to Lowell at all. One explanation was the lack of other money-making alternatives. Employment of women outside of the home had traditionally been limited to domestic service and school teaching. Neither of these occupations paid well and the former was considered socially degrading. Mill work, therefore, however toilsome, offered girls an opportunity to save some money and gain a certain sense of independence. As one of the girls wrote: the work was preferable "to going out as 'hired help.'" To persons who had seldom had money of their own, the Lowell wages could seem substantial, and, since most farm girls were accustomed to laboring from sunrise to sunset, the Lowell hours did not at first appear too excessive. There was also the excitement of being away from home, meeting new people, and broadening one's social and intellectual horizons. Some girls came to Lowell to work because of the glowing reports about it; most of these persons, however, were quickly disillusioned. For, as Lucy Larcom recalled, "instead of an Arcadia, they found a place of matter-of-fact toil . . . ."

While Lowell's paternalism was not altogether altruistic in the beginning, it became less so as years went on. The financial success of the Boston Associates led them to expand, and this encouraged others to establish competing textile plants. The competition in turn caused the price of cotton cloth to drop. In order to maintain high dividends, therefore, the Lowell owners pressured the factory managers to speed up production and reduce labor costs. As early as 1830, both the hours of labor and the number of machines tended by each operative were increased. In 1834 and again in 1836, wages were cut from fifteen to twenty-five per cent. Piece rates were introduced as a method of making the girls work harder, and premiums were granted to overseers who were able to increase production. By the 1840's workers were tending four looms, yet earning no more than girls who had tended one or two a decade earlier. The outward appearance of paternalistic benevolence continued to impress visitors, but to the workers this pretense only made the actual conditions seem that much grimmer. Just how far Lowell had fallen from its image as an industrial utopia was indicated in a candid statement by one of the mill managers in the mid-1840's: "I regard my workpeople just as I regard my machinery. So long as they can do my work for what I choose to pay them, I keep them, getting out of them all I can."

The girls did not accept the harsh dictates of the increasingly impersonal corporation without opposition. In 1834—the same year that Chevalier, Davy Crockett, Harriet Martineau, and other visitors were extoling Lowell and its operatives—about 2,000 girls went out on strike in protest of the announced wage cuts. The strike failed of its purpose, as was also true of an 1836 turnout, but discontent continued to mount. "As our fathers resisted unto blood the lordly avarice of the British ministry," proclaimed one of the 1836 strikers, "so we, their daughters, never will wear the yoke which has been prepared for us."

By the 1840's the labor agitation at Lowell took on broader dimensions. At the beginning of that decade, Orestes Brownson, New England's radical gadfly, published two widely circulated essays on "The Laboring Classes," attacking the Lowell system. "We pass through our manufacturing villages," he wrote, "most of them appear neat and flourishing. The operatives are well dressed, and we are told, well paid. They are said to be healthy and happy." But this, he related, was "the fair side of the picture; the side exhibited to distinguished visitors. There is a dark side, moral as well as physical. Of the common operatives, few, if any, by their wages, acquire a competence . . . . The great mass wear out their health, spirits, and morals, without becoming one whit better off than when they commenced labor. The bills of mortality in these factory villages are not striking, we admit, for the girls when they can toil no longer go home to die. The average life—working life, we mean—of the girls that come to Lowell . . . is only about three years. What becomes of them then? Few of them ever marry; fewer still ever return to their native places with reputations unimpaired."

And what of the proceeds of this labor? Brownson asked rhetorically. They go to a man who is "one of our city nabobs, revelling in luxury; or he is a member of our legislature, enacting laws to put money in his own pocket; or he is a member of Congress, contending for a high Tariff to tax the poor for the benefit of the rich; or in these times [period of depression] he is shedding crocodile tears over the deplorable condition of the poor laborer, while he docks his wages twenty-five per cent."

Brownson's statements were somewhat of an exaggeration, particularly in his references to the loss of moral virtue by the operatives. But his analysis in "The Laboring Classes," which Arthur Schlesinger, Jr. has called "the best study of the workings of society written by an American before the Civil War," does show a keen understanding of the detrimental effects the machine and the corporation were having on the economic relationships between classes. Like Marx, he saw that a person operating a machine owned by another was in an inherently unequal position.

Most Americans of the day were horrified by Brownson's radical perceptions. Harriet Farley, the editor of the *Lowell Offering,* attacked Brownson indignantly for his charges of immorality, though glossing over the economic issues. An apologist for the mill owners, Miss Farley claimed that the operatives should have nothing to do with wages and hours. Others, however, while seldom going as far as Brownson in the extent of their attacks on the capitalist system, were far less willing than the *Offering* editor to leave such things as wages and hours in the hands of all-wise overseers and directors. Sarah Bagley, Mary Emerson, Huldah Stone, and other factory girls organized the Lowell Female Reform Association in 1844 to work for humanitarian causes and especially for a ten-hour work day. In October, 1845, they began publication of the *Voice of Industry,* a labor paper directed at both bread and butter issues and general panaceas. Two months later the celebrated *Lowell Offering* ceased publication—its stories of moral uplift no longer relevant to the operatives.

In the mid-forties, led by the Reform Association, the fight for the ten-hour day dominated labor interest. The progressive labor speed-up at Lowell over the years made the twelve- to thirteen-hour day particularly onerous. Only with sufficient leisure, it was argued, could the workers better themselves through education and other means of self-improvement. Several long petitions demanding ten-hour legislation were sent by the Lowell workers to the Massachusetts Legislature. Failing to move that body, workers began organizing, not just at Lowell, but throughout New England. Innumerable conventions were held; other labor papers were started; new petitions were gotten up; a number of strikes occurred and even open violence erupted in some mill towns. But all such efforts proved unsuccessful, and conditions continued to deteriorate. In 1848 the Lowell Female Reform Association, which had previously been renamed the Labor Reform League of New England, ceased to function. That same year, a new sharp wage cut further depressed the laboring conditions.

Up to the 1840's one of the chief characteristics of the factory population at Lowell had been its temporary nature. Girls had come for one or two years, saved some money, and then left to marry, or to teach school, or to find a new life in the West. The factory owners had even defended the long hours of labor on the basis of the short periods of employment.

But by the 1840's the mobile New England mill girls were being driven from the factories by the long hours, low wages, rigid discipline, and speeded-up labor. Those who remained were becoming a more permanent factory population dependent on industrial employment for a meagre subsistence. As the more ambitious and skillful girls departed Lowell, the famed labor system rapidly broke down. At first the owners and managers tried to perpetuate it, sending out agents greater and greater distances to bring in new girls and paying a bounty to these functionaries for each additional recruit. But even these "slave" runs (as they were known to the laborers) failed to maintain the system. From the mid-1840's on, it was increasingly abandoned in favor of hiring immigrants streaming in from Ireland, Germany, and French Canada. The end result was that Lowell, which had been the New World exemplar of industrial utopia, became instead just one of many competing mill towns, successful because of the ruthless exploitation of an increasingly permanent and stratified labor force.

A fitting requiem for the end of the idyll that Lowell had once symbolized would be Melville's story "The Tartarus of Maids." Though set in a paper mill, the tale was clearly an attack on the farm-girl labor system made famous at Lowell. It opens with a man traveling toward the paper mill across the "bright farms and sunny meadows" of New England. But his route takes him "among bleak hills," between the "cloven walls of haggard rock," through the gorge at "Black Notch" and into the hollow known as "the Devil's Dungeon" cut by the "Blood River." Arriving at the mill in weather that has turned biting cold, the man enters to encounter "rows of blank-looking counters" behind which "sat rows of blank-looking girls, with blank, white folders in their blank hands, all blankly folding blank paper." The air inside this mill was hot and "swam with . . . fine, poisonous particles, which from all sides darted . . . into the lungs." The only sound was "the low, steady overruling hum of the iron animals. The human voice was banished from the spot. Machinery—that vaunted slave of humanity—here stood menially served by human beings, who served mutely and cringingly as the salve serves the Sultan. The girls did not so much seem accessory wheels to the general machinery as mere cogs to the wheels."

Dominating the factory and the pride of the owners was "the great machine" that made the paper. Gazing "upon this inflexible iron animal" the visitor was awestruck: "Always, more or less, machinery of this ponderous, elaborate sort strikes, in some moods, strange dread into the human heart, as some living, panting Behemoth might. But what made the thing I saw so specially terrible to me was the metallic necessity, the unbudging fatality which governed it . . . . I stood spell-bound and wandering in my soul. Before my eyes—there passing in slow procession along the wheeling cylinders, I seemed to see, glued to the pallied incipience of the pulp, the yet more pallid faces of all the pallid girls I had eyed that day. Slowly, mournfully, beseechingly, yet unresistingly, they gleamed along, their agony dimly outlined on the imperfect paper . . . ."

Having inspected the factory, the stranger inquires why it is that the operatives regardless of age "are indiscriminately called girls, never women?" He is told that it is because they are unmarried. "For our factory here, we will not have married women; they are apt to be off-and-on too much. We want none but steady workers: twelve hours to the day, day after day, through the three hundred and sixty-five days, excepting Sundays, Thanksgiving, and Fast-days." With a silent bow to the "pale virginity" of the maids, the traveler rides away from the artificial world of the "iron animals" back to "inscrutable nature," exclaiming as he passes out of the Devil's Dungeon—"Oh! Tartarus of Maids!"

This industrial nightmare of Melville's, far-fetched though it obviously was, came closer to capturing the realities of New England factory labor than the more frequently asserted rhapsodic ideal. The things that Melville depicted—the idea of labor as a commodity, the relentless pressure of the methodical machinery, the dehumanizing effects of factory work, the unhealthy conditions, the removal from nature—were all actualities in Lowell of the 1840's.

If the story of Lowell were exceptional, its deterioration, however significant symbolically, would be of little note in the history of Jacksonian America. But Lowell was not the exception. The revolutions in industry and transportation that set the era off from previous periods created a growing class of wage workers who in most instances labored long hours for low wages in ill-ventilated and poorly lighted mills, and lived in crowded, filthy housing. In fact, the unusual thing about Lowell was its distinctly unproletarian appearance in the early years. Most other factory towns, in New England and elsewhere, seem almost to have been conceived in squalor, never experiencing a utopian phase.

In Pennsylvania, for instance, William A. Sullivan, the historian of industrial workers in that state, found that the growth of manufactures from 1820 to 1840 was remarkable, but that the factory operative did not benefit from the increased prosperity. The apparent opportunities for the workingman to improve his status were largely ficticious. "By the thousands," Sullivan wrote, "workers flocked to the cities to meet the demands of new industries, and these urban manufacturing centers teemed with masses of land-less job-hunting wage earners."

Poverty and overcrowding became widespread in Penn-sylvania, particularly in the major cities. A citizen's com-mittee in the summer of 1832 examined living conditions in Philadelphia's largely working-class Upper Delaware Ward. "The result of this investigation shows," the com-mittee reported, "that the whole number of tenements is sixty-four; total number of inhabitants, four hundred and seventy-three. Of these, there are thirty tenements con-taining fifty-five families, and two hundred and fifty-three individuals, that have not the accommodation of a privy for their use." A Pittsburgh physician, testifying before a Pennsylvania Senate committee investigating industrial conditions in 1837, related that "factory children generally . . . live in confined, narrow, ill-ventilated rooms and cel-lars, among the poorest of the poor, in old frame houses where the atmosphere is peculiarly bad, highly impregnated with putrid miasmata, arising from the offals and miserable population—each family having, in many instances, only a single room for all purposes of life."

The same 1837 Senate committee hearing also revealed that children under twelve made up about one-fifth of the work force in Pennsylvania's textile factories. Their wages ranged from as low as 12½ cents a week to 75 cents. Women workers, who also made up a sizable portion of the textile labor force, received slightly higher pay, any-where from 50 cents to $2.62 per week. The large num-bers of women and children in these mills made it diffi-cult on occasions for men to find employment. As at Lowell, there was a marked tendency for wages to be re-duced, hours lengthened, and the tempo of the machine work increased. The engineer in the steam-powered mills, an observer in the mid-1830's reported, "regulates the speed of the machinery, and all the operatives, adults and children must keep pace with it." "A strict and almost superstitious discipline," another contemporary witness claimed, "is necessary to keep this vast instrument going for one single day."

Pennsylvania's textile mills were largely urban, which helps explain the overcrowding and unhealthy conditions. Philadelphia more than doubled in size from 1820 to 1840, while Pittsburgh trebled its population in those decades. The result of this rapid growth was an almost indescribable congestion.

But even in the rural areas of the state the factories and foundries were far from faultless. A good example was the iron industry. Pennsylvania was the leading iron-producing state in the pre-Civil War years. In 1840 the state's furnaces, according to the United States Census, were turning out nearly 100,000 tons of pig and cast iron annually. Mines, mills, furnaces, and forges were found throughout the state with heavy concentrations in the southeastern district and in the west, in the counties around Pittsburgh. The great majority of these iron works were in the countryside, but the iron worker's rural existence was not a fruitful one. The labor was hard and sometimes dangerous. Most iron works were in company-owned towns. Sullivan states that the life of the iron worker was not unlike that of the medieval serf. "He looked to the ironmaster for his job and his home; made his purchases at his store, and often found himself heavily in debt and his freedom seriously circumscribed by his obligations to him."

In general, Pennsylvania workers felt a sense of degradation and a loss of status and independence. "Those who are toiling day after day," lamented a Philadelphia laborer in 1827, "spending their strength, and wasting their health in the production of wealth are doomed not only to poverty with all its attendant inconvenience, but even to contempt." Observing the debasement of the working class, a conservative Philadelphia newspaper, *Poulson's Daily American Advertiser,* suggested on August 18, 1830, that although "laboring in the field or in a workshop cannot confer any distinction . . . it ought not be a degradation."

Laborers in New York, the nation's wealthiest and most populous state, experienced a similar sense of loss when they confronted the changes wrought by industrialization. An 1829 writer for the prolabor New York *Evening Journal* bemoaned that "although the Mechanics are the most useful and powerful body of men in the community, and . . . as respectable as any other class, they are . . . considered in many points inferior . . . . Is it a stain upon the character to gain an honest livelihood by useful industry? . . . There are more real gentlemen among this than any other class." Defensive statements such as the above were increasingly common in the labor and prolabor writings of the 1820's and 1830's.

New York City was a major industrial center by the late twenties, producing everything from ships and pianos to shoes and precision instruments. One of the most extensive and exploitative of the city's industries was the ready-made clothing business. Numerous sweatshops thrived on the labor of women needleworkers. A reformer of the early thirties estimated that a seamstress working a full week could, on the average, sew nine shirts. Prices paid for this work varied from six to ten cents per shirt, giving these women a weekly wage of fifty-four to ninety cents a week "for the incessant application of a human body, during thirteen or fourteen hours a day, for the payment of rent, the purchase of food, clothes, drink, soap, candles and fuel!" In 1833 a New York doctor attributed the growth of prostitution in the city to the poor pay in the needle trades: "My profession affords me many and unpleasant opportunities of knowing the wants of those unfortunate females, who try to earn an honest subsistence by the needle, and to witness the struggles often made by honest pride and destitution. *I could site many instances of young and even middle-aged women, who have been 'lost to virtue,' apparently by no other cause than the lowness of wages and* THE ABSOLUTE IMPOSSIBILITY OF PROCURING THE NECESSARIES OF LIFE BY HONEST INDUSTRY."

The population of New York stood at about 123,000 in 1820. By 1840 there were over 312,000 inhabitants. As in Philadelphia, house construction did not keep pace with the rising population. Consequently, more and more persons were forced to occupy less and less space. All available housing was put to use from cellars to attics, and by the late 1830's New York had a tenement-house population that could rival any of Europe for density, filth, disease, crime, and vice. The most notorious of the city's slums was a section known as the Five Points, formed by the intersection of Orange, Cross, and Anthony streets. Here thousands of persons, according to a shocked foreign visitor, lived "under circumstances more wantonly injurious than the despotism of Russia." "Death, langour, listlessness, and disease" hovered everywhere. At the center of this area was a large building that once had been a brewery, but which by the late thirties housed over a thousand persons—"the rudest and most degraded portion of the population of New York."

A large percentage of New York's slum dwellers were foreign born. From the Revolution up to the mid-1820's, immigration had not been a major factor in American growth, and those who had arrived were readily absorbed into the expanding economy without causing drastic wage reductions. This lack of large-scale immigration had been a democratizing force that had allowed a fairly homogeneous middle-class society to develop. However, during the thirties, at a time when equality seemed triumphant, immigration sharply increased, causing fluid social and economic conditions to move toward a state of social stratification. In 1828, while Jackson was defeating Adams for the presidency, 30,000 registered passengers entered the United States. Four years later, over 50,000 aliens arrived, and the annual total was to fall below that figure only twice before the Civil War. All told, nearly 600,000 immigrants came to America in the 1830's.

Such massive immigration presented a clear challenge to this country's democratic ideals. Not only did immigrants form a growing slum population like that in New York's Five Points, but they also came to constitute a more than adequate supply of cheap labor to man the expanding factories, perform heavy construction work, and fill the need for domestic servants and other menials. Although the most detrimental social and economic effects of heavy immigration in pre-Civil War America were experienced in the 1840's and 1850's, already in the 1830's there was evidence that the labor of foreigners was a major factor undermining organized labor and causing wages to drop for both native and immigrant workers. Not only political nativists, but Americans as a whole, regarded recent immigrants as inferior beings, little better than the Negro. Even an Irish emigrant agent felt compelled to warn his fellow countrymen not to be too proud and think that America was a land of freedom where one man was as good as another. "It is true," he wrote, "that at the legal tribunal and at the voting booth all are equal, but there the equality ends . . . . Every demand for a fellowship with respectable society, grounded upon the *law* of the land, will be rejected with contempt . . . ." This class-conscious feeling together with the obvious economic inferiority of the majority of immigrants presented a strong challenge to egalitarian America.

Then, as now, it was relatively easy for the middle-class

majority to overlook the galling poverty of the laboring classes, foreign and native-born alike. American attitudes toward the poor had been shaped by Protestant individualism and an agrarian environment in which scarcity of labor had been a traditional problem. It was assumed that destitution stemmed from individual indolence and ineptitude, and that any honest and willing worker could find employment at a decent wage if he so desired. The existence of relatively cheap lands in the frontier West served to further ease consciences disturbed by growing signs of poverty in the industrializing Northeast. Most Americans thought that as long as unsettled lands existed, an impoverished urban proletariat could be avoided. Therefore, even when poverty was seen, it was believed to be a passing aberration.

The ease with which even the most astute of citizens could ignore the problems of penury was well illustrated by the attitudes of the economist and manufacturing champion Mathew Carey. Up until 1827 Carey had always assumed that industrialism was a panacea which would benefit all classes, including workers. In that year, however, he happened to discover that Philadelphia's poor rates were rapidly rising. After a thorough investigation, he found to his dismay that many workers in Philadelphia did not receive a subsistence wage. This discovery led him to become a crusader on behalf of the poor and one of the first middle-class reformers to realize that most industrial poverty was not the result of dissipation or laziness. There was, wrote Carey in an 1833 pamphlet, a large class of laborers "whose services are so inadequately remunerated, owing to the excess of labour beyond the demand for it, that they can barely support themselves while in good health and fully employed, and, of course when sick or unemployed, must perish, unless relieved by charitable individuals, benevolent societies, or the guardians of the poor." He came to realize that even labor-saving machines were not an unmixed blessing, as they often drove down wages, caused unemployment, or both.

Carey's investigations revealed that even more oppressed than the factory operative was the unskilled common laborer who was employed mostly to do construction work on buildings, canals, turnpikes, and railways. Such jobs were hard, poorly paid, unhealthy, and seasonal. Carey gave the following description of canal construction in 1833: "Thousands of our labouring people travel hundreds of miles in quest of employment on canals, at 62, 75, and 87 cents per day, paying a dollar and a half or two dollars a week for their board, leaving families behind, depending on them for support. They labour frequently in marshy grounds which destroys their health, often irrevocably. They return to their poor families—with ruined constitutions, with a sorry pittance, most laboriously earned, and take to their beds sick and unable to work. Hundreds are swept off annually, many of them leaving numerous and helpless families. Notwithstanding their wretched fate, their places are quickly supplied by others, although death stares them in the face."

The declining condition of factory workers and common laborers in the era was not an isolated northeastern phenomenon. Richard Wade, in a pioneering study of Pittsburgh, Cincinnati, Lexington, Louisville, and St. Louis from 1790 to 1830, has shown that all of the problems plaguing the eastern wage earner also affected the rapidly growing working class in these western cities. Due to labor scarcity, wages in the West were slightly higher than in the East, but long hours, child and female labor, inadequate housing, and a general sense of declining status were all present. Even organized labor movements appeared in the West by 1830. These movements tried to secure the ten-hour day and to generally bolster the position of the working class.

As in the East, these efforts met with little success.

In addition to a wage-earning class, "whose numerical strength," in Wade's words, "outstripped that of all other groups," these transmontane cities also had a large transient population of common laborers. Boatmen, wagoners, canal workers, and drifters formed an unruly substrata of urban society in the West. Whole city blocks of boarding houses, cheap hotels, grog shops, and whorehouses existed to serve and exploit this element of the population. The life of this class was easily as precarious as that of the eastern day-laborer. Employment was seasonal, wages were minimal, living conditions were wretched. In such an environment, East or West, men soon lost their will to succeed. Physical energy became sapped; the mind dulled. In this state it was a short step to heavy drinking, vice, or crime.

While the worst working conditions in the 1820's and 1830's were experienced by common laborers and factory operatives, those most vocal about deteriorating conditions were the skilled artisans working in the apprenticeship system. From the colonial period through the early nineteenth century, trained craftsmen such as shoemakers, tailors, cabinetmakers, and coopers had enjoyed an esteemed position in American society. The apprenticeship system allowed for a good deal of vertical mobility. Ranks from apprentice through journeyman to master were like rungs of a ladder to be climbed by the ambitious artisan. Workers within this system did not think of themselves as wage earners; they sold a product, not their labor. The medieval concept of a fair price and a just wage still prevailed. Employers and employees shared the labor and the profits, generally working in the same small shop and producing goods ordered for the local market.

By the mid-1820's this harmonious system was breaking down. Rapid transportation, a rising urban population, enlarged credit, increased mechanization, and industrialization economically altered America. Canals, turnpikes, and, later, railways created larger markets for manufactured goods; this in turn helped induce revolutionary changes in craft-shop production. Organizational entrepreneurs moved into controling positions in most of the apprenticeship trades. These middlemen bought and sold goods in quantity over a broad area. Often they would distribute raw materials to craft shops and buy back the finished products. Master craftsmen, no longer producing for a fixed local market, were forced to sell to the middleman at the latter's price. This in turn drove the master to reduce his production costs, including labor. The brunt of this pressure was born by the journeymen and apprentices employed by the master. Piecework was introduced to speed up production and decrease expenses. It was then possible for masters to hire less skilled, and therefore cheaper, workers. Women, children, recent immigrants, and even prisoners, leased by various jails, began to replace skilled artisans. Under such pressure the entire apprenticeship system deteriorated.

To journeymen accustomed to a respected and reasonably remunerated job with the prospect of future advancement, the collapse of the traditional system came as a shock. They became insecure about their status and were made aware for the first time that their interests, in the words of the New York journeymen printers, were *"separate and in some respects opposite to those of the employers . . . ."* The sense of outrage was evidenced in much of the labor writing and rhetoric of the twenties and thirties. "Monopolists and capitalists," claimed an 1830 labor newspaper, have usurped the rights of mechanics, "abridging their privileges by opposing them in their business with the advantage of a large capital." "Men who are no mechanics," the article continued, "are engaged in mechanical concerns . . . at the expense of the interest of the legitimate mechanics; and in many cases, preventing the industrious, enterprising, but perhaps indigent mechanic, from following his trade to advantage, or from following it at all."

The major labor movements, unionist and political, that appeared almost simultaneously with the triumph of the Jacksonian Democrats, derived most of their strength from the frustrations of the artisan class, though by the thirties many factory operatives and other less-skilled laborers had also organized. Trade associations and Working Men's political parties from Maine to Missouri arose to demand the ten-hour day, abolishment of imprisonment for debt, free public education, an end to compulsory unpaid attendance at state militia drills, elimination of special privileges and monopolies, reform of banking, and prohibition of paper money.

Many of these labor objectives won broad support. They were in the interests not only of skilled workers and more common laborers, but also of small shopkeepers and businessmen, professional persons, and most individuals not directly aided by some special privilege. The numerous grievances against vested interests made many middle-class persons espouse the reform measures initiated by labor. Several of the demands were taken up by the two major parties and enacted into law. In most states imprisonment for minor debts was abolished; militia laws were modified so as to be less burdensome to workers. The drive for free public education became one of the leading reforms of the age, and, although not everywhere enacted, major gains were made in the period. The attack against monopolies and privileged banking institutions became a national crusade, centered in the Democratic Party and leading to the defeat of the "Monster" Bank of the United States. In addition, various states passed free banking and general incorporation laws to limit the circulation of paper bills of small denomination, and to remove banks and other companies from the realm of chartered monopolies.[1] Such measures marked a gain for the workingman and a general advance for free enterprise.

Seeing that Working Men's political parties generally ceased their independent existence at about the same time that the Democratic Party began its antimonopoly crusade, Arthur Schlesinger, Jr. in his *Age of Jackson* (1945) concluded that the workers had aligned with the Democrats and that the major egalitarian thrust of Jacksonian Democracy stemmed in large part from the working class.

However, a great deal of subsequent scholarship has shown that there was nothing like a major shift of allegiance by laborers from their own organizations to the Democratic Party. In fact, as a recent labor historian writes: "What is of special interest was the tendency of labor leaders not only *not* to affiliate with the Democrats but, if anything, to attack that party with special vindictiveness, as though to counteract the belief inculcated by some Jacksonians that their party was peculiarly close to the laboring man."

One influential interpretation which emerged in criticism of Schlesinger has been the so-called "entrepreneurial" thesis. Writers of this school have argued that America was basically a middle-class, capitalist society and that what disagreement did exist was largely a struggle between established entrepreneurs and expectant capitalists. This, they contend, explains the broad support labor-sponsored measures received. The keynote of labor's demands was not a proletarian hatred of capitalist society, but the desire for an equal chance to share the fruits of capitalism. Capitalist consensus, not class conflict, is central to this thesis.

---

[1] Ten-hour day legislation was passed in some states by the 1840's. But since the ten-hour principle applied only in the absence of contracts, the effects of such laws were minimal. Van Buren's 1840 executive proclamation of a ten-hour day for federal employees on public works was equally ineffectual.

The above interpretation implies that the workers, like most Americans, were basically optimistic men-on-the-make, confident of the chance to strike it rich. Yet if this were completely true one would assume that the enactment of the major labor-supported measures would have somewhat allayed worker frustrations, improved their social and economic position, and reduced class antagonisms. This, however, was not the case. Achievements such as abolishment of imprisonment for debt or more democratic banking laws in no way checked the overall economic changes which were reducing formerly independent craftsmen to the level of wage earners and turning temporary factory workers into a permanent proletariat.

By the mid-thirties, labor activities had become more militant and were directed more specifically at bread and butter issues—higher wages and shorter hours. "The time has now arrived," proclaimed the leader of the New York Typographical Association in 1833, "for the mechanics of our city to arise in their strength and determine that they will no longer submit to the thraldom which they have patiently borne for many years, nor suffer employers to appropriate an undue share of the avails of the labourer to his disadvantage." "The social, civil, and intellectual condition of the laboring classes," complained a report drawn up by the Trades' Union National Convention of 1834, exhibits "the most unequal and unjustifiable distribution of the produce of labor, thus operating to produce a humiliating servile dependency, incompatible with the inherent natural equality of man . . . ."

A recognition of the antagonistic nature of the employee-employer relationship affected almost all workers by the mid-1830's. More than two hundred active trade associations flourished with an estimated membership of anywhere from 100,000 to 300,000. Over 160 strikes occurred between 1833 and 1837, most of which were for higher wages. Noting the mounting evidence of class strife, the Philadelphia *Public Ledger,* October 11, 1837, looked longingly back upon a time "not far distant, when we heard nothing from American presses, about classes and *distinctions* of *rank.* Then, all occupations were considered *equally honorably* [sic], and distinctions between *individuals* were founded, not in trades and *professions,* but in character and conduct."

The relationship between labor and capital was further strained by the antagonistic reactions of employers and much of the middle-class public to organized workers. Employers' associations were formed to bar from employment, as one such association stated, "any man who is known to be a member of . . . any society which has for its object the direction of terms or prices for which workmen shall engage themselves." In addition to such blacklisting, the conservative courts of several states held that any combination of workers aimed at raising wages or shortening hours through united action constituted an illegal conspiracy.

Another frequently used managerial tactic (one which has been employed throughout much of this nation's labor history) was to persuade the public that unions and their leaders were un-American and therefore undesirable. Unions, claimed the probusiness *New York Commercial Advertiser* in 1836, "are based upon the same principles as the pernicious Trade Unions in England, and in almost every case, we are informed, they are managed and controlled by foreigners." A textile mill owner testified similarly before the Pennsylvania Senate in 1837 that the only evil in the factory system of that state was the Trades' Unions which had "been imported to this country by English and Irish men within a few years, and which had a tendency to destroy the good feeling which has, heretofore, existed between the employer and the workmen in this country."

Such tactics were effective. The gains of organized labor were slight, and in the long run illusory, since not only employers, but general economic trends undermined labor's position. To make matters worse, the prosperous conditions that had buoyed up the labor movement came to an abrupt end in the depression of 1837 which lasted through the early 1840's. Unemployment and reduced wages became the general rule; organized labor collapsed. Both skilled and unskilled workers were left without effective organizations at a time when continued industrial expansion and increased immigration depressed the entire wage-earning class and widened the gap between classes. "The actual condition of the workingman today," pointed out Orestes Brownson in "The Laboring Classes" (1840), "is not so good as it was fifty years ago . . . . Fifty years ago," he romanticized, "health and industrious habits, constituted no mean stock in trade, and with them almost any man might aspire to competence and independence. But it is so no longer. The wilderness has receded and already the new lands are beyond the reach of the mere laborer, and the employer has him at his mercy."

Nineteenth-century social thinkers from Marx to Durkheim saw one of the most detrimental effects of industrialization to be the progressive alienation of the worker from himself and society. Over a decade before Marx began exploring this problem, however, the most brilliant analyst of American society, Alexis de Tocqueville, had already noted this phenomenon as a basic danger confronting the New World Republic. The disintegration of the whole man through the division of labor was carefully observed by Tocqueville: "When a workman is unceasingly and exclusively engaged in the fabrication of one thing, he ultimately does his work with singular dexterity; but at the same time he loses the general faculty of applying his mind to the direction of the work. He every day becomes more adroit and less industrious; so that it may be said of him that in proportion as the workman improves the man is degraded. What can be expected of a man who has spent twenty years of his life making heads of pins? And to what can that mighty human intelligence . . . be applied by him, except it be to investigate the best method of making pins' heads? When a workman has spent a considerable portion of his existence in this manner, his thoughts are for ever set upon the object of his daily toil; his body has contracted certain habits, which it can never shake off: in a word, he no longer belongs to himself, but to the calling which he has chosen . . . ."

The decline of skilled crafts and the division of labor within industry diminished the workers' sense of creativity, self-esteem, and social status. Laborers had turned to generally middle-class reforms in the hope of reintegrating themselves into society. This should not be surprising, given the alternatives in Jacksonian America. Marx had not yet written; Owen's experiments were not widely known; Fourier was an unfamiliar figure. Laissez-faire economics promised to free the worker from the unnatural restraints of legislative privilege.

This does not prove, however, that workers were middle-class or even budding entrepreneurs. In fact the surprising thing was the extent of radicalism in Jacksonian labor thought. In a recent book, *Most Uncommon Jacksonians* (1967), Edward Pessen, after examining the social philosophies of both trade union leaders and labor politicians, concludes that "the leaders of the Jacksonian labor movement were radicals . . . . How else describe men who believed American society to be torn with social conflict, disfigured by the misery of the masses, and dominated by a greedy elite whose power over every aspect of American life was based on private property?" Not only did forthright radicals such as Thomas Skidmore, the New York leader of the early Working Men's Party, speak out against private property, but most other labor leaders also expressed this position. "All on arriving at adult age," editorialized George Henry Evans in his *Working Man's Advocate,* November 14, 1829, "are entitled to equal property." "Without labor there can be no property," stated a Philadelphia Working Men's party leader. "The accumulation of the wealth of society in the hands of a few individuals," claimed John Ferral, a union leader, "is subversive of the rights of men."

The radical thought of labor leaders was part of the growing awareness of wage earners that their interests as a class were separate and distinct from other social classes. If one could speak of a Jacksonian consensus in which it was believed that Americans—guided by divine providence and deriving moral virtue from their republican institutions and closeness to Nature—could accomplish great things through individual determination, then clearly a growing segment of working men, women, and children had a vague sense of being outside of such a consensus. For them, the price of industrialization was increasing social stratification, alienation, and exploitation. Benevolent capitalism, as first conceived at Lowell and other early industrial centers, had rapidly become a contradiction of terms.

CHAPTER FIVE

"Eager after Aristocratic Distinctions"

O<small>N</small> F<small>EBRUARY</small> 27 <small>OF THE DEPRESSION YEAR</small> 1840, Philip Hone, the wealthy and fashionable New York diarist, attended an elaborate costume ball held at the Henry Brevoort mansion on the corner of Fifth Avenue and Ninth Street. "Never before," he confessed, "has New York witnessed a fancy ball so splendidly gotten up, in better taste, or more successfully carried through." According to James Gordon Bennett's *New York Herald,* the first paper to specialize in society-page coverage, nearly six hundred of the "*elites* of this country were there." Devoting the entire first page to the affair, the *Herald* reporter described the costumes of the various Caesars, Sultans, Hamlets, Othellos, and Queen Victorias. One dress, it was stated, cost more than $2,500. Excellent food and wine were in abundance, served by an army of liveried servants. This gala event, summarized the characteristically overexuberant *Herald* writer, "created a greater sensation in the fashionable world than any thing of the kind since the creation of the world, or the fall of beauteous woman, or the frolic of old Noah, after he left the ark and took to wine and drinking."

The summer previous to the Brevoort ball, Hone had been present at another scene of fashionable frolic—the summer season at Saratoga Springs. On August 12, 1839, Hone wrote in his diary: "This is the meridian of the Saratoga season. All the world is here: politicians and dandies; cabinet ministers and ministers of the gospel; officeholders and office-seekers; humbuggers and humbugged; fortune-hunters and hunters of woodcock; anxious mothers and lovely daughters . . . ." Hone was staying at the elegant United States Hotel of which he wrote: "no watering-place in this or any other country can boast of a pleasanter establishment." Present at the time were a varied group of planters, merchants, manufacturers, speculators, and politicians—the elite of North, South, and West, uniting, in Hone's words, "as in one brilliant focus the talent, intelligence, and civic virtues of the various parts of the country."

Costly parties and exclusive summer resorts were only two of the many types of conspicuous display indicative of a class of persons attempting to assert their superiority in an ostensibly democratic society. The United States, of course, had no permanent and hereditary ranks and distinctions. There was no titled nobility who possessed definite legal and social privileges. Government was allegedly democratic; there was no established church; laws of primogeniture and entail had long been abolished; and the road to social and economic advancement was, at least in theory, open to everyone. Yet despite this (or perhaps because of it), the era witnessed distinct efforts on the part of many persons to claim higher rank than their fellow citizens.

American equality was that of legal rights and not a general condition of society. Recognizable class distinctions existed in all sections of the country and were recognized by all ranks of society. The terms "lady" and "gentleman" were used discriminately. As Lyman Beecher's eldest daughter Catherine noted in an 1842 tract, "we . . . call persons who have wealth and education 'ladies,' and persons who have no education, and labour for a support 'women.'" A "lady," she added, would feel offended to be called a "woman" since "persons whom she regards as below herself are so-called." In both the fictional and nonfictional writings of the period quite sharp class demarcations were taken for granted. A praiseful 1832 guidebook for prospective immigrants warned that "there is *society* in America, as in any part of the world. But notwithstanding all the theoretical notions of Republican equality, society there has its *grades,* and every one must expect to take his own proper rank." The following year the touring English captain, Thomas Hamilton, made a similar observation: "It is the fashion to call the United States the land of liberty and equality. If the term equality be understood simply as implying, that there exists no privileged order in America, the assertion, though not strictly true, may pass. In any wider acceptation it is mere nonsense. There is quite as much practical equality in Liverpool as New York. The magnates of the Exchange do not strut less proudly in the latter city than in the former; nor are the wives and daughters more backward in supporting their pretensions. In such matters legislative enactments can do nothing."

That many persons, in the words of Francis Grund, should have "a very nice taste for artificial distinctions" in an age of rampant theoretical democracy is not surprising. Americans were a striving people living in an era of accelerated economic change. They were motivated by both economic rewards and social ones. The ability to rise to higher levels seemed greater than ever before because of the more rapid rate of economic growth. It was only natural, then, that a democracy of opportunity helped create an aristocracy of achievement.

The social order in Jacksonian America—as were the economic and political arrangements—was in flux. Numerous new opportunists flooded the ranks of the rich, making it difficult for the established families of colonial times to preserve their preeminence. Political deference to one's "betters" had given way to baiting of the "gentleman" running for office on the basis of his social status. Both Whigs and Democrats by the mid-thirties claimed to represent the people, and no aspiring politician dared oppose equal political rights. There was no Tory or even Federalist party to represent the upper classes.

Other traditional bulwarks of aristocracy had been similarly weakened. The church—one of the mainstays of privileged social order in Europe, and to a lesser extent in colonial America—had everywhere been disestablished by the 1820's. Since church sects competed with one another for membership and support, most tended to cater to popular, egalitarian sentiment.

Nor was there a large aristocratic officer class in the United States Army, though increasingly sons of southern planters were attending West Point and an officer elite was emerging. But the military was not highly regarded in America, and the proliferation of colonels, majors, and captains in the ragged state militia systems served effectively to undermine the prestige of military titles.

Despite these democratizing factors, certain prestigious families preserved distinguished reputations into the age of the common man. Such families would include: the Winthrops, Dudleys, and Saltonstalls of Massachusetts; the Browns of Rhode Island; the Van Rensselaers, Livingstons, and Schuylers of New York; the Logans, Cadwaladers, and Pembertons of Philadelphia; the Carrolls of Baltimore; the Carters, Randolphs, and Lees of Virginia; the Pinckneys, Hugers, and Butlers of South Carolina. In fact virtually every community from Portland, Maine to

New Orleans had its local elite, whether landed or mercantile. Many such families intermarried and were very exclusive in their social life.

Family fortunes, however, in an expanding economy and in a society in which wealth was subdivided among many heirs, seldom could be maintained for more than a few generations. Even when kept intact, what would have been a fortune in the colonial era was not considered great wealth in the more affluent age of Jackson. Wealth in the form of land was undermined by the availability of newer and often better lands to the West and by the absence of entail and primogeniture. There was a marked tendency in the seaboard states for great landed properties to decline in the Jacksonian period. Two of the largest estates in America, the 80,000-acre holdings of Charles Carroll of Carrollton and the nearly 700,000 ancient acres of Stephen Van Rensselaer, III, both were broken up following the deaths of their owners in 1832 and 1839 respectively. Basil Hall, the visiting British naval captain, noticed signs of this collapse of the landed gentry when sailing up the Hudson in 1827: "The steep shores are generally wooded, and every where studded with villages, or with single country houses, belonging to the ancient aristocracy, which is now rapidly withering away in that part of the country, as it has already done almost every where else in America, to the great exultation of the people, before the blighting tempest of democracy."

However, respectable old families could and often did preserve themselves by uniting with the parvenu in marriage—trading respectability for money. When an old Boston aristocrat was asked in the mid-1830's why he had consented to have his daughter marry a *nouveau riche* rustic, he replied: "I give my daughter to any man who will come to Boston and have wit enough to make a hundred thousand in six years." City directories of wealthy citizens, such as Moses Yale Beach's *Wealth and Biography,* comprising brief sketches of New Yorkers worth over $100,000, served as marriage guides for mercenary mothers. Arranged marriages between rich but new families and threadbare but respectable old families became more and more frequent during the 1830's and 1840's. Such marriages, according to one moralist, were "coldblooded calculations, determinations for vulgar display, meretricious shows from beginning to end. There is slender opportunity or desire for election in them. They are managed, directed, and accomplished by and through ambitious mothers and their thoroughly disciplined daughters."

Not only did marriage alliances join old and new wealth, there were also intersectional alliances.[1] Henry Brevoort, Jr., son of a wealthy New York City landholder, married Laura Carson of Charleston; New York Roosevelts frequently married Barnwells of Charleston; in 1846 John Jacob Astor's grandson married the daughter of Thomas L. Gibbes of South Carolina; Governor Henry A. Wise of Virginia wed the daughter of a Philadelphia Sergeant. Such matches were often cemented, sometimes by chance and sometimes by arrangement, at fashionable summer resorts such as Saratoga Springs or Newport.

Besides marriage as a means of preserving the respectable status of an old family, many persons of traditional wealth were able to keep pace with changing times through diversifying their investments. It has been conventional for historians in speaking of pre-Civil War society to draw a contrast between mercantile and landholding families on the one hand and capitalist-industrialists on the other, implying that these groups—representing an "old" and a "new" aristocracy—were diametrically opposed to one

---

[1] The intersectional nature of fashionable society in America lasted until the eve of the Civil War, though signs of its breakdown were evident in the 1850's.

another. In practice, however, there seldom was such a clear-cut split between types of wealth. In Boston, for instance, the capital to found and expand the textile industry came largely from merchants. And although all respectable shipping families did not immediately support Lowell, Appleton, Lawrence, and the other Boston Associates from the beginning, they did not hold out long, once the success of textile production became known. In 1829 the cleavage between Boston merchants and manufacturers could be said to have come to an end when Thomas H. Perkins and Ebenezer Francis, two of the last wealthy merchants to withhold their capital from industry, invested in the Lowell Manufacturing Company and the Appleton Company. Similarly in New York, the names of wealthy old families—Van Rensselaers, Schuylers, Aspinwalls, Phelps, and Howlands—could be found backing railroads and manufactures along with the newly rich Astors, Vanderbilts, Coopers, Colgates, and Cornells. Even in the South, though there was much less diversification of wealth, nothing like an inseparable barrier existed between the urban factor and the rural planter.

In short, wealth itself was what mattered most, not whether it was "old" or "new." As Emerson noted in 1834, "In a former age men of might were men of will; now they are men of wealth." Wealth has always been associated with gentlemanliness and provides a distinguishing feature in itself, while at the same time bestowing on its possessor the leisure and means to cultivate social refinements. The lack of permanent hereditary distinctions made material success that much more important. "Americans," lamented the moralizing Reverend Isaac Fidler in 1832, "boast of their skill in money-making; and as it is the only standard of dignity, and nobility, and worth, in that country, they endeavour to obtain it by every possible means." "The avarice of an American in general," observed a Britisher, "is nothing more than the passion of ambition directed to the acquisition of wealth as the only means of attaining distinction in the state of society in which he is placed."

The accumulation of great wealth was not, of course, confined to any one class or place. The ability to become rich was basic to the American dream and underlay the widely accepted belief in progress. Society was viewed as an inclined plane upon which the only acceptable direction was up. Tocqueville sensed this quality of American life in which no one was "devoid of a yearning desire to rise . . . ." "To clear," he wrote, "to till, and to transform the vast uninhabited continent which is his domain, the American requires the daily support of an energetic passion; that passion can only be the love of wealth; the passion for wealth is therefore not reprobated in America, . . . it is held in honor." Since wealth was the chief symbol of status, most Americans not only felt compelled to achieve it but also to spend it conspicuously as a sign of their success. As a Whig journal, *The American Review* (January, 1845), complained: "We are ashamed of any thing but affluence, and when we cannot make an appearance, or furnish entertainments as showy as the richest, we will do nothing."

The emphasis on individual achievement ran counter to the concept of equality, but in expanding America "equality of opportunity" was the slogan that supposedly reconciled these conflicting ideals. The dream of rags-to-riches ("from log cabin to White House") meant, in effect, unobstructed freedom of enterprise within a framework of democratic political rights. "True republicanism," as one contemporary put it, "requires that every man shall have an equal chance—that every man shall be free to become as unequal as he can." As long as America remained a land of small farmers, craftsmen, and merchants, there did not appear to be any contradiction between the notion of equality of opportunity and a general equality of condition.

In the first decade and a half after the War of 1812 it had seemed to many Americans that the economic millennium, like the spiritual one, was close at hand. New businesses were opening; new cities were developing; new methods of transportation were conquering distance; new lands were available. Labor was still relatively scarce and therefore, judged by European standards, well paid. Opportunity seemed to be everywhere, and it appeared that America would be able to create the ideal of eighteenth-century thought—an enterprising, intelligent, homogeneous, classless, republican population.

Yet increasingly after about 1830, several major factors reversed the trend toward economic equality and worked toward the stratification of society. First, the great increase in industrialization and the tendency toward specialized large-scale production in factories made a hierarchical economic system that sharply separated employee from employer. Second, the great growth of immigration together with the increased employment of women and children undermined organized labor and created an easily exploitable labor force. Third, rapid urbanization intensified social stratification and created a more impersonal environment. Fourth, the consolidation of the South's plantation system greatly reduced social mobility in that region. Fifth, the recession of the frontier and the increased agricultural specialization made the West less and less of a "safety-valve."

The very equality of opportunity of which Americans boasted was actually one of the major factors helping to create a new economic aristocracy. Jacksonian democracy came to resemble a Darwinian world of cutthroat competition in which opportunism was given free scope and in which the weakest went to the wall. The old aristocracy of heredity was either replaced by, or amalgamated with, a new oligarchy of wealth. But because the forms of republicanism were respected and the dream of rags-to-riches was cultivated, republic-loving Americans, priding themselves on having abolished the aristocratic trappings of the Old World, for a time deluded themselves into believing that the grossest economic inequalities had nothing to do with class distinctions.

Yet distinctions there were, and yearly they became more pronounced. One of the results of the somewhat sudden appearance of great wealth was the development in the urban East, and to a lesser extent in the cities of the South and West, of High Society—a society-page class partially dependent on conspicuous consumption as a means of gaining social notoriety. The way of life of this wealthy set distinguished it from the rest of society far more markedly than did the less ostentatious life of any earlier elite. High Society was an overt manifestation of caste. It was active and conspicuous, stemming from the rise of plutocratic wealth coupled with the decline of the class of gentry. It was based on the snobbish need that newly enriched individuals felt in order to have a secure sense of identity and place.

The first requisite for high standing in fashionable society was wealth, though wealth alone was never enough. Neither John Jacob Astor nor Cornelius Vanderbilt, two of the richest of the pre-Civil War plutocrats, were ever at ease or welcomed in the drawing rooms of Society. Their sons and daughters, however, became leading figures in High Society. Examples of the two-generation conversion from plutocrat to aristocrat can be gleaned from the sketches in Beach's *Wealth and Biography*. A representative case was that of John W. Moffat and his son. Beach listed the elder Moffat as "the founder of the celebrated 'Life Pills and Phoenix Bitters,' by the manufacture and sale of which he has amassed his present fortune." The son William B. Moffat, on the other hand, was described as possessing "that greatest mine of wealth—a thorough and complete education—his recent travels in Europe have so polished the jewel that its owner must shine in future years as a distinguished man."

For some, it was possible to win social acceptance in a single generation. Philip Hone's career well illustrates this. The son of a carpenter, Hone, together with his brother John, started out in the auction business in 1797, at a time when New York City was beginning its spectacular rise to commercial dominance in America. In 1821 after twenty-four years of uninterrupted money-making, Hone, who was just approaching forty, retired from business with a handsome fortune. Thereafter, he consciously devoted himself to becoming a gentleman. He traveled widely in Europe and taught himself to appreciate art, literature, history, and fine wines and foods. He rapidly became one of the central figures in the richest and most distinguished New York society. His imposing manners, aristocratic tastes, patronage of the arts, and love of the traditional, all ingratiated him with fashionable society. Besides being one of the founders of the Italian Opera in 1833 and of New York's exclusive Union Club in 1836, he also became a governor of the New York Hospital, and a trustee of Columbia and of the Bloomingdale Insane Asylum. A Whig in politics, an Episcopalian in religion, Hone lived to see his children marry into the old Dutch aristocracy. When he died in 1851, the *Herald* wrote that "in the fashionable world Mr. Hone held a high rank in the prime of life, being always considered a leader of the *ton*. Indeed, it has been said that if an order of nobility had existed in this country, Mr. Hone would have claimed the right of being numbered in their ranks. His bearing, though courteous toward his fellow citizens, was aristocratic and self-confident, and when any of the foreign nobility or other aristocracy visited our shores, they received his hospitality . . . ."

Etiquette books of the period aimed specifically at transforming persons of wealth into ladies and gentlemen. As the well-born authoress Catharine M. Sedgwick wrote: "I have seen it gravely stated by some writers on manners that 'it takes three generations to make a gentleman.' This is too slow a process in these days of accelerated movement . . . . You have it in your power to fit yourselves by cultivation of your minds and refinement of your manners for intercourse, on equal terms, with the best society in our land." Over one-hundred books on social decorum were published between Jackson's 1828 election and the Civil War. According to Arthur M. Schlesinger, Sr., books of etiquette were nearly as popular in the frontier West as in the effete East. These behavior books aimed not only at teaching manners, but also at instilling class distinctions and appealing to social snobbery. The popularity of the Earl of Chesterfield's maxims on behavior was a good example. Lord Chesterfield's work, with its chivalric ethic of courtly self-gratification, went through many American editions. *The American Chesterfield* (1827), a condensed manual with what American editors considered the improprieties expurgated, became the most popular etiquette book of the age, teaching a highly aristocratic moral code.

American writers on manners, though usually more moralistic than the English Earl, also assumed and encouraged a class-structured society. "Never at any time," warned *The Laws of Etiquette* (1836), "whether at a formal or a familiar dinner party, commit the impropriety of talking to a servant: nor ever address any remark about one of them to one of the party. Nothing can be more ill-bred. You merely ask for what you want in a grave and civil tone, and wait with patience till your order is obeyed." This same source in another section recommended in relation to servants to "avoid the dangerous and common error of exercising too great humanity in action. No servant, from the time of the first Gibeonite downwards, has ever had too much labour imposed upon him; while thousands have been ruined by the mistaken kindness of their masters." In thousands of elaborately observed usages the ladies and gentlemen of High Society distinguished themselves from the commonalty.

Appearing almost simultaneously with the rise of High Society, and in part responsible for its growth, was society-page reporting. Although newspapers had on occasion written of fashionable doings previous to the 1830's, it was in this decade that the society page made its appearance as a regular feature of the city newspaper. The Scottish immigrant James Gordon Bennett—the founder of *The New York Herald* in 1835—announced in the edition of March 17, 1837, that: "No one ever attempted till now to bring out the graces, the polish, the elegancies, the bright and airy attributes of social life . . . . Our purpose has been, and is, to give to the highest society of New York a life, a variety, a piquancy, a brilliancy, an originality that will entirely outstrip the worn out races of Europe." Bennett and his reporters began giving feature coverage to balls, parties, charities, fashions, Saratoga and Newport, and other social doings. He picked up servants' gossip and published it; on occasion he threatened a scandalous report unless a *Herald* reporter was admitted into a fashionable function. It was in this manner that one of Bennett's writers gained access to the Brevoort ball of 1840. Bennett's techniques were highly successful and widely imitated. By the mid-forties the young Walt Whitman was complaining in the columns of the *Brooklyn Eagle* that newspapers spent too much time informing readers "whether A eats roast beef or Graham bread." Despite complaints, however, the rise of such reporting did a great deal to increase society consciousness among all classes.

Besides the press, the real custodians of the world of

fashion were women. In fact the rise of High Society was directly related to the growing leisure of wealthy women and to the honored place they held. Where a woman is kept in the kitchen (or factory), society is impossible. But in this period an idle wife became a partial measure of a man's success. Most men, regardless of the size of their fortune, continued to work, which gave them something in common with virtually every other American male. But for the wives and daughters of the well-to-do, a way of life developed that was strikingly different from the American norm. As an English traveler remarked in the early 1840's: "The professional man may be on the very best of terms with the blacksmith, but ten chances to one if the daughters of the professional man know the blacksmith's daughters, or if they would acknowledge it if they did." Anna Mowatt in her delightful social satire *Fashion* (1845) has the French maid tell the footman: "Monsieur is a man of business— Madame is lady of fashion. Monsieur make the money,— Madame spend it. Monsieur nobody at all,—Madame, everybody altogether."

The wives and daughters of wealth were America's first leisure class. Having sufficient servants to take care of ordinary domestic duties and not being allowed to follow a profession or even a serious intellectual pursuit, aristocratic ladies gave an inordinate amount of attention to fashion. "It is women," stated the drawing-room author N. P. Willis, "who regulate the style of living, dispense hospitalities, exclusively manage society, control clergymen and churches, regulate the schemes of benevolence, patronize and influence the Arts, pronounce upon Operas and foreign novelties . . . ." The custom developed among fashionable women in the eastern cities of the thirties to set aside one morning each week as a time to receive callers. On that occasion, according to an observer, "you will find her enshrined in all that is grand and costly; her door guarded by servants, whose formal ushering will kill within you all hope of unaffected and kindly intercourse; her parlors glittering with all she can possibly accumulate that is *recherché,* . . . and her own person arrayed with all the solicitude of splendor that morning dress allows, and sometimes something more."

The way in which fashionable women attempted to keep America safe from democracy was clearly illustrated by the well-known Peggy Eaton affair. Peggy, the vivacious and beautiful daughter of a Washington tavern keeper, after a youthful marriage to a man named Timberlake who died at sea, had wed Jackson's close friend and Secretary of War, John Eaton. She was immediately snubbed by the ladies of Washington society; whereupon Jackson, himself a widower whose late wife had been slandered in the 1828 campaign, came to her defense. This, however, was to no avail. Not only did the other cabinet members' wives, led by Mrs. Calhoun, refuse to admit Peggy to social functions, but even Jackson's own niece and White House hostess, Mrs. Andrew Jackson Donelson, would not consent to call upon Mrs. Eaton, though custom and the President demanded that she do so. The affair dragged on, but in the end the people's President proved unsuccessful in democratizing the capital's drawing rooms. So steadfast were the Washington ladies in their opposition to receiving the War Secretary's wife into society, that Jackson dissolved the cabinet partly because of this issue. After the Eaton affair, the social power of women was seldom contested.

But society in America consisted of much more than feminine snobbery and garish displays of wealth. Men of money not only aspired to social distinction, they also clamored for positions of economic (and sometimes political) power. This was the masculine side of society. In many cities such men comprised something of a ruling elite, dominating the social, economic, and political life of the community.

One of the best examples of this type of power and prestige was the position of the Boston Associates in that city. Composed of about forty families, the Associates had become by the late 1820's a cohesive clique, having achieved a leading position in the business affairs of Massachusetts and much of New England. Most members of the Associates were persons of both wealth and birth. However, two relatively upstart families—the Appletons and the Lawrences—had gained acceptance and powerful positions among them by backing Francis Cabot Lowell's Waltham experiment in the early years when the textile industry was still considered a risky investment. By the late 1820's the ranks of investors had tightened to the exclusion of outsiders. Virtually all of the stockholders were related by blood or marriage. When initially establishing the Boston Manufacturing Company, Lowell had turned for support to his Cabot relatives and to his wife's brothers, the Jacksons. Even Nathan Appleton could claim a distant kinship with the Lowells. A few of the leading families had preserved their high status from the colonial era, notably the Saltonstalls, Winthrops, and Endicotts. Others, such as the Lowells, Cabots, Lees, Perkinses, Jacksons, Amorys, and Searses, had gained their initial wealth through commercial activities during and after the Revolution. Intermarriage cemented these various families into a closed class, and after the 1820's few newcomers entered the inner circle.

These Boston capitalists, though most noted for their factories at Lowell, had a commanding interest in virtually all of the major textile mills of northern New England. By 1850 they controlled about one-fifth of the cotton spindleage in the country. In addition, they dominated the merchant shipping of Boston and had extensive interests in real estate, insurance, banking, railroads, and other business. All of the Boston banks but one, the Commonwealth, were managed by the Associates, and, during the panic of 1837, that bank collapsed, leaving the credit structure solely in the Associates' hands. Even the Boston branch of the Bank of the United States, before the demise of that institution, was headed by William Appleton. Similarly the major railroads radiating from Boston—the Boston and Albany, the Boston and Maine, the Connecticut River, the Boston and Lowell, the Nashua and Lowell, the Taunton Branch, and the Western Railroad—were directed by the Associates. As William Appleton noted approvingly: "We find that the proprietors of the more than twenty millions of capital invested in the roads terminating in the Boston area are, to a very considerable extent, the same."

The extensive economic interests of these Boston businessmen caused them to pay close attention to politics. Here too they played a major role, sometimes serving in the Massachusetts General Court or in Congress at Washington, but more often they were ably represented by such politicans as Daniel Webster and Edward Everett. In Boston they generally controled the Mayoralty and the Common Council, and in the state they or their allies dominated the Whig party until that organization broke up over the slavery issue. Theodore Parker, writing with only slight exaggeration on the political power of the Associates, stated in 1845 that "this class is the controlling one in politics. It mainly enacts the laws of this state and the nation; makes them serve its turn . . . . It buys up legislators . . . . It can manufacture governors, senators, judges to suit its purposes, as easily as it can manufacture cotton cloth . . . . This class owns the machinery of society . . . ships, factories, shops, water privileges."

As might be expected, these Boston nabobs also played a significant part in shaping the religious and educational life of the community. The majority of the Associates were Unitarian and rewarded well the genteel clergy who presented an undemanding and comfortable creed. Ministers who would make of Unitarianism an idealistic faith that asked of its adherants a moral commitment to social justice found little favor. Theodore Parker, who used the pulpit to attack both southern slavery and the northern merchant-manufacturing aristocracy, was told by Thomas Gold Appleton through one of his parishioners that: "We will make Boston too hot for you." They nearly succeeded. In a like manner Amos Lawrence refused in 1842 to give any further funds to Harvard Divinity School because of what he termed the "bad influence" of Emerson, Parker, and Orestes Brownson. "Mr. Emerson," he wrote, "is an amiable man, but who . . . would choose him to instruct them in the ways of wisdom?"

Harvard College was a favorite charity for the Boston elite. Teaching a traditional curriculum with a strong emphasis on moral orthodoxy, Harvard seemed a suitable bulwark against violent social change. Even some western colleges were supported for the same reason. It also became fashionable for the Boston elite to finance and serve as trustees and directors for such institutions as the Massachusetts Historical Society, the Boston Athenaeum, King's Chapel, and the Massachusetts General Hospital.

Living in elegant mansions centered about Boston Common, or on Beacon Hill, or Back Bay, these magnates shared an exclusive way of life. Their common views, values, and activities gave them a strong sense of security, and allowed them to dominate the fashionable society of Boston, while at the same time enjoying the realities of prosperity, prestige, and power.

Philadelphia and Baltimore societies were similar to Boston's in that they too were tightly knit and dependent on both birth and wealth. New York, Pittsburgh, Cincinnati, and Chicago offered greater opportunities for the newcomer to achieve wealth and social recognition. But in all these urban communities, the industrial revolution, in conjunction with gains in commercial wealth and urban land values, was creating a powerful and prestigious class of financial magnates in the midst of democratic America. A limited group in most areas was acquiring wealth, social recognition, and a good deal of control over the nation's manufacturing, transportation, and commercial facilities.

Class lines were sharpening in urban America, whether in the East or the reputedly more egalitarian West. "We have our castes of society," stated an 1826 Pittsburgh directory, "graduated and divided with as much regard to rank and dignity as the most scrupulous Hindoos maintain, in defense of their religious prejudices." Between the "classes," this source continued, "there are lines of demarcation drawn, wide, distinct, and not to be violated with impunity." Four years later, an English traveler was surprised on arriving in Lexington to discover that "there was a greater number of handsome coaches, some of them with servants in livery, than I have met with, excepting at Charleston. There is an air of wealth about the place."

Richard Wade, in his careful study of Ohio Valley cities up to 1830, concluded that with each passing decade "class divisions deepened, and the sense of neighborliness and intimacy weakened . . . . Everywhere growth and expansion intensified earlier stratification." Economic life in the western cities became more specialized and impersonal; this in turn, according to Wade, not only increased class stratification but also insulated the classes from one another. With each new generation the wealthy and prestigious families became more sheltered and classbound. From private schools and colleges the sons and daughters of the rich moved naturally into social and business relationships based on class and family ties and held together by exclusive clubs such as the Quintilian Society of Pittsburgh, the Whig and Union Philosophical societies of Lexington, or the Philomatians and Erophebics in Cincinnati. Thus, rather than being a democratizing force, the urbanization of the West only saw the class distinctions and sense of status, so marked in the eastern cities, repeated in these newer communities.

In the South, town life was less significant, though no less stratified. Charleston appeared to many visitors to be the most aristocratic city in the Union. "The society of Charleston," wrote a foreign traveler in 1833, "is the best I have met with in my travels, whether on this or your side of the Atlantic. In respect to finish, the elegance of manners, it leaves nothing to be desired . . . ." Visible signs of class abounded—spacious town houses surrounded by walls and gardens, carriages bearing coats of arms, servants in livery, exclusive clubs such as the St. Cecilia Society and the Jockey Club.

But Charleston society, unlike that of northern cities, was dominated by a planter oligarchy whose wealth was derived from agriculture. This was a significant fact found throughout the South. The cities that developed as the cotton plantation economy spread through the lower South in the first decades of the nineteenth century grew only after the farm lands were settled and developed as adjuncts to agriculture. The hegemony of the great slave holders extended alike over urban and rural classes. While in the North newly rich merchants and industrialists were attaining positions of honor and power, in the South such persons played a secondary and supporting role to that of the planters—the real custodians of social and political power.

A good deal has been written in the past generation attempting to prove that the antebellum South was not a deviant from democracy. Fletcher M. Green in an article on "Democracy in the Old South," *Journal of Southern*

History (February, 1946), demonstrated that the South experienced extensions of white manhood suffrage and increased political participation at about the same time as the North. Subsequent scholarship by Frank Owsley, Charles Sydnor, Clement Eaton, Richard McCormick, and Dewey Grantham, Jr. has sustained Green's findings and also stressed the significance of the middle-class and the importance of the Whig party in the South.

These analyses are important and have done much to correct the traditional view of an oligarchic South confronting a democratic North in the decades preceding the Civil War. But the picture presented by such writings may well be an overcorrective. Stanley Elkins and Eric McKitrick, in a persuasive 1954 article, have argued that although the political tone of the South became democratic during the Jacksonian period, this did not mean a lessening of the power of the planting aristocracy as a class. The planters themselves made the concession of adopting a democratic political style, but their leadership was never seriously at issue. "The primary demands of Southern society," these scholars concluded, "were still the demands of its landed, slave-holding nucleus of social and political power."

Elkins and McKitrick explain the paradox of a democratic rhetoric clothing an aristocratic order by referring to two factors which typified the development of the old Southwest. First, there was present from the beginning a class of planters whose leadership the people were accustomed to accept. Second, there was an agrarian economy of limited diversity which presented few problems that could not be handled in time-honored ways by the traditional leaders. Successful southern agriculture, based as it was on a slave-labor system, was run by routine and custom. This gave credence to the image of the South as a changeless, static society. The increasing defensiveness of Southerners over their peculiar institution further hard-

ened this view and even created a hostility to innovation.[2]
Thus, though the South continued to speak of common-
man democracy, the vital reform movements sweeping the
North in these years were absent (except for prohibition).
There were no organized interests opposed to the slave-
plantation system and neither compromise, dissent, nor
public debate on issues were common features of the political life. In short, southern politics were essentially un-
democratic. Proslavery thinkers from Dew and Calhoun
to Fitzhugh preached the necessity of aristocracy, pointing to the cultures of Greece, Rome, and the Italian city
states as examples of the need for both slaves and an
elite. Black slavery had become the institution on which
southern aristocracy rested.

One should keep in mind, of course, that in the antebellum period many of the wealthiest planters were as parvenu
as some of the northern nabobs. It was only in the 1830's
that the frontier flux of land grabbing and fortune building
had begun to give way to the stable plantation system.
One-generation aristocrats such as the Davises of Mississippi, Howell Cobb of Georgia, or the Aikens of South
Carolina were not uncommon, and up until the Civil War
it was still possible for the strong, striving, and lucky individual to become a great planter. The fictional career of
Thomas Sutpen in William Faulkner's *Absalom, Absalom*
is well within the realm of historical possibility.

Yet mobility in the South was less than in the North
because there were fewer enterprises open to the ambitious
individual. Throughout much of the South, cotton was

[2]A good illustration of this was the fact that several southern cities had ordinances prohibiting the use of steam power. This situation led the pioneering
southern advocate of manufacturing, William Gregg, to ask concerning such an
ordinance in Charleston: "Why are our mechanics forbid to use it [steam power]
in this city? This power is withheld lest the smoke of an engine should disturb
the delicate nerves of an agriculturist; or the noise of the mechanic's hammer
should break upon the slumber of a real estate holder, or importing merchant,
while he is indulging in fanciful dreams . . . ."

indeed king, and success in its planting depended on large, fertile farms with a substantial slave labor force to work them. Gradually the rich silt-loamed lands of Georgia, Alabama, and Mississippi and the alluvial bottom lands of the Mississippi and Yazoo delta were absorbed by the great cotton planters. As one contemporary noted, "the thrifty swallow up the property of the thriftless."

Social status was visible in the South; it rested on the number of slaves one owned, the quantity and quality of one's land, and the stateliness of one's mansion. Only about one white family in four had a proprietary interest in slavery, and of these five-sevenths owned fewer than nine slaves. The major planters, those who possessed fifty or more slaves and eight hundred or more acres, never composed as much as one per cent of the white population. In 1850, for instance, the Census listed fewer than eight thousand holders of fifty or more slaves out of a total white population of over six million. But despite the fact that the great slave holders made up only a tiny fraction of the population, they dominated southern society and represented the social ideal of the South. They were the models of social aspiration for the ambitious small planter or town merchant. As Eugene D. Genovese noted in his study of *The Political Economy of Slavery:* "The planters commanded Southern politics and set the tone of social life. Theirs was an aristocratic, antibourgeois spirit with values and mores emphasizing family and status, a strong code of honor, and aspirations to luxury, ease, and accomplishment."

Francis Grund, always an astute observer of American life, asked in 1839: "Is it not strange . . . that in a country which more than any other convinces one of the vanity of human pursuits,—in which wealth, honour, and distinction are mere bubbles floating on the surface of society,—men should be more eager after aristocratic distinctions, than where these are founded on an historical basis, and in accordance with the customs of the people?" Such, he found, was the case; the America he saw was "characterized by a spirit of exclusiveness and persecution unknown in any other country."

While Grund was not alone in analyzing the aristocratic pretensions and sharp gradations of the age, few historians until recently have taken this evidence seriously. Instead, they have appropriated Tocqueville's characterization of the 1830's as an era of equality. This is understandable because most traditional studies have focused on the politics of the period and have assumed that great democratic advances were being made by the common man. Recent historiography, however, has begun to emphasize the increasing urbanization, industrialization, and social stratification of the second quarter of the nineteenth century. Furthermore, modern political studies have shown that nothing like a democratic revolution occurred during the period, and that common-man rhetoric could, and frequently did, clothe demagogic power. In the light of this evidence, is it not time that historians scrap labels like "The Age of the Common Man" or "The Age of Egalitarianism"? Such generalizing concepts do not clarify the realities of the era, and their continued use serves only to misdirect students and scholars alike.

CHAPTER SIX

"Pernicious Tendency
of the Parties"

Addressing himself to the nature of major party politics in 1831, the labor spokesman Stephen Simpson claimed that "nothing of a public nature, at the present era, is so worthy of the attention of the people as the fallacious structure and pernicious tendency of the parties now in vogue . . . ." These parties, he contended, neither advanced the good of the nation nor the prosperity of the people, but blindly ministered "to the avarice, ambition, or pride of some temporary idol, who is worshipped one day and immolated on the next." The basic problem with existing parties, Simpson concluded, was their absence of principle; composed of men with "conflicting views, irreconcilable principles, and incompetent minds," these *personal parties* sacrificed honesty to expediency, "truth to self-interest, patriotism to ambition, and public virtue to private aggrandizement." Honest people, "duped by unprincipled leaders," supported such unholy factions. "Lured on by the cant of party, the slang of affected patriotism, and the hollow promise of patronage, men have closed their eyes as well as their understandings to the deception of the game, which made use of them and their interests for the sheer and exclusive benefit of an aspiring demagogue . . . ."

Less radical observers made similar observations. Early in 1832, Alexis de Tocqueville, drawing on conversations he had held with the historian Jared Sparks and the lawyer John Latrobe, made a distinction between "great" political parties and "small" parties. The former were "those concerned with principles and not their consequences, with general questions and not with particular cases, with ideas and not men . . . ." The little parties, on the other hand, were "without political faith, their characters are consistent and stamped with a blatant selfishness shown in all their acts . . . . Their language is violent, their progress timid and uncertain. The means they employ are wretched, as is the end they seek . . . ." Tocqueville believed that the Federalists and Jeffersonian Republicans had been great parties. Those of Jackson's time, however, were decidedly not. "I cannot conceive," he wrote, "a more wretched sight in the world than that presented by the different coteries (they do not deserve the name of parties) which now divide the Union. In broad daylight one sees in their breasts the excitement of all the little shameful passions . . . . As for the country's interest, no one thinks about it, and if it is referred to, that is for form's sake. The parties put it at the head of their deed of association, just as our fathers printed 'by royal permission' on the first page of their books."

The implications of Simpson's and Tocqueville's analyses are that the two major parties of the Jacksonian period were basically similar, being nonideological coalitions, concerned more with success at the polls than with broad principles. Other contemporaries supported such an evaluation. The seemingly bitter political rivalries in the United States, explained James Fenimore Cooper to an English readership, were "essentially, nothing more than two great

parties, struggling for place, and who adopted different
politics about as much for the purpose of opposition as for
any other reason." The contest between Jackson and
Adams in 1828 was, Cooper insisted, "altogether one of
men." "It would be impossible to say," stated Nicholas
Biddle in 1831, a year before he became the center of the
period's most divisive political controversy, "what is the
political belief of those who support the administration, or
of those who attack it . . . . Political emotions have scope
only over the details of administration and not over its
principles." That same year, a Baltimore lawyer described
politics as based solely on "questions of personalities. There
are those who have got power and those who want to have
it; the 'ins' and 'outs.' " Even the editors of the major
Jacksonian journal, the *Democratic Review,* admitted that
the "violence of party" obscured the basic "democratic
spirit and sentiment" shared by both parties.

Partisan politicians, of course, took party divisions more
seriously and saw them as being based on differences of
principle. The Democrats liked to picture themselves as the
representatives of the *people* arrayed against the aristocratic champions of privilege. Many Jacksonians believed
that the party divisions of the 1830's were a continuation
of conflicts dating back to before the Revolution. "It was
first Tory," wrote a leader of the Massachusetts Democratic
Party in 1834, "then Federalist, then no party, then amal-
gamation, then National Republican, now Whig, and the
next name they assume perhaps will be republican or
democrat. But by whatever name they reorganize themselves, the true democracy of the country, the producing
classes, ought to be able to distinguish the enemy . . . .
They are composed in general of all those who are, or who
believe themselves to be favored by some adventitious
circumstances of fortune. They are those . . . who have
contrived to live without labor, or who hope one day to

do so, and must consequently live on the labor of others."

National Republicans and, later, Whigs did much to further the image of the Democrats as the party of the masses. Their attacks charged the Jacksonians with Jacobinism; Democrats were denounced as "atheists, infidels, agrarians, incendiaries, men who were without religion and honesty, who desire to pull down all that is venerable in the institutions of the country, to seize the property of the rich, and divide it among the poor." Such assaults had the effect of convincing many people that parties were divided on class lines and that the Democrats were indeed the party of the people.

By the late 1830's, however, the Whigs had learned the shortcomings of such a political approach. "The cry of aristocracy takes with certain folks," noted one Whig leader, "and there is no way to meet it but to clamor louder than our adversaries . . . ." In the Log Cabin campaign of 1840 they out-democratized the Democrats in convincing the majority of voters that General William Henry Harrison, the hero of Tippecanoe who was descended from one of the first families of Virginia and who lived in a fine house along the Ohio, was the true man of the people. Instead of calling the Democrats leveling radicals, the Whigs attacked the incumbent Van Buren as an aristocrat who lived luxuriously in the White House at the people's expense.

Another supposed difference of principle that Whig politicians seized upon involved the authority of the chief executive. As President, Jackson was convinced that he, more than any other elected official, represented the will of the people. Almost single-handedly he transformed the nature of the presidency. His use of the veto more than all previous presidents combined, his setting aside of Supreme Court rulings, his removal of individual office holders, his strong stand against the South Carolina nullifiers, his implementation of an aggressive Indian policy, all served to increase presidential power. But to the Whigs this was an unconstitutional usurpation of congressional rights. The strength of President Jackson, proclaimed Henry Clay in an 1837 Senate speech, "is felt from one extremity to the other of this vast republic. By means of principles which he has introduced and innovations which he has made in our institutions, alas! but too much countenanced by Congress and a confiding people, he exercises uncontrolled the power of the State . . . . He has swept over the Government, during the last eight years, like a tropical tornado. Every department exhibits traces of the ravages of the storm."

The Whigs developed the theory that their party had been organized, in the words of an 1844 pamphleteer, to protect "this nation and its posterity against the imperious claims and mischievous precedents made and established by General Jackson and his partisans, to the enlargement of Executive and the diminution of Legislative power." The fundamental principle of the Whigs, this writer emphasized, was "the assertion of the Representative Privilege against the Executive Prerogative. No candid and sincere lover of rational, republican liberty . . . can contemplate the encroachments of Executive power . . . without a resolute revolt in his heart against that whole system of political domination by which these encroachments have been compassed. That there was not such universal revolt may be set down to the artful engendering and skillful control of faction whereby men's passions have mastered their judgments."

This contemporary debate as to whether political parties represented pragmatic coalitions of ambitious office seekers or principled men trying to implement coherent ideologies has been mirrored by more than a century of conflicting historical interpretations. The first scholarly study of

Jacksonian politics, written by George Tucker in 1857, characterized the party of Jackson as an opportunistic grouping of "Federalists and Democrats, Bank and anti-Bank, tariff and anti-tariff partisans, friends and enemies of internal improvements." Such an interpretation would appear again and again. Recently, for instance, a noted authority has written that "the political parties of the Jacksonian period, like those of today, were made up of congeries of conflicting interests."

Many other historians, however, have seen the politics of the era in terms of broad ideological clashes in which parties represented the interests of classes or sections or both. Generally speaking, those scholars who have interpreted the party battles of the period in ideological terms have associated the triumph of Jackson with the rise of democracy; whereas historians who have found party splits to be essentially over means and not ends have de-emphasized the democratizing role of Jackson and his party. It will be useful, therefore, to critically evaluate the ways in which historians have interpreted the relationship of democracy to the period's politics.

The association of Jackson's party with democracy, as the concept "Jacksonian democracy" implies, was one not unfamiliar to contemporaries. The Jacksonians more than any previous party, wrote Francis Grund in 1837, "carried out the principles of pure democracy." Grund described General Jackson as "the idol of the people whose interests he endeavoured to protect by every act of his military and political life." "I never saw such a crowd here before," exclaimed the disapproving Daniel Webster at Jackson's 1829 Inauguration. "Persons have come from five hundred miles to see General Jackson, *and they really seem to think that the country is rescued from some dreadful danger!*" To Jackson's loyal supporters such was the case. The Old

Hero was taking up, where Jefferson had left off, the fight of the people against the ever-present dangers of aristocracy, privilege, and corruption.

Yet nineteenth-century scholarship subsequent to the Jacksonian period was slow to explore the connections claimed by contemporaries between the Democratic party and democracy. With a few notable exceptions such as the staunch Jacksonian George Bancroft, the writing of American history through most of the nineteenth century was dominated by persons friendly neither to Jackson nor to the common-man concepts of democracy. James Parton and William Graham Sumner, the first serious biographers of Jackson, and Herman E. von Holst and James Schouler, authors of general histories covering the period, were generally critical of Jackson the man and saw the movement he led as a corrupt, demoralizing, and demagogic force in American life that led directly to Grantism and Tweedism.

In the last fifteen years of the century, however, younger scholars, sympathetic to the reform impulses of their own day, began re-evaluating the course of the country's democratic growth. In 1886, Richard T. Ely, the pioneer labor economist, published *The Labor Movement in America* in which he argued that a close association had existed between the aspirations of common laborers and farmers and the policies of the Jacksonian movement. "The Democratic party from 1829 to 1841," he wrote, "was more truly a workingmen's party than has been the case with any other great party in our history." Ely's assessment had little influence in its day, though in retrospect it can be seen as a harbinger of certain twentieth-century interpretations.

The historian who did the most to reorient the writing of our nation's history in terms favorable to Jackson and democracy was Frederick Jackson Turner. The presentation of his famous 1893 paper on "The Significance of the Frontier in American History," signaled the beginning of a democratic agrarian school of scholars that dominated the writing of Jacksonian history for the next forty years. Where Turner led, twentieth-century historians such as William McDonald, John Spencer Bassett, Vernon L. Parrington, and Claude Bowers soon followed.

By the 1920's this prodemocratic, pro-Jackson revisionism was triumphant. In that decade the typical textbook interpretation of the Jacksonian era ran something like this: First, it was assumed that American history from its beginnings had been characterized by conservative and democratic forces and that the struggle between these opposing forces shaped the oscillating course of the nation's development. Thus, while the Revolution and Jefferson's victory in 1800 had been democratic triumphs, replacement of the Articles of Confederation by the Constitution and the dominance of the Federalists in the 1790's were, it was assumed, conservative victories.

In the so-called "Era of Good Feelings" following the War of 1812, things had become somewhat muddled, but the basic divisions in society remained the same, and by the election of 1824 had come back into focus. In that election Andrew Jackson had emerged on the political scene, representing the new western states with their frontier democratic tendencies. Cheated of his rightful triumph due to the political machinations of John Quincy Adams and Henry Clay, Jackson's democratic legions prepared for 1828. Jackson's victory that year marked the second American Revolution. The party of privilege was replaced by the reign of the people, symbolized by the muddy-booted, commonman constituents present at Jackson's Inaugural. It was a victory of West over East, democracy over conservatism, equal opportunity over special privilege, agrarianism over capitalism, honest labor over aristocratic leisure.

To cement this triumph, Jackson ousted entrenched office holders and rewarded the party faithful by introducing the "democratic" spoils system. In an Homeric struggle, Jackson succeeded in destroying the chief bastion of privilege, the "Monster" Bank of the United States. In 1835 with the death of John Marshall, the Judicial branch of government—the last stronghold of Federalism—was democratized; the good Jacksonian Roger B. Taney became the new Chief Justice and quickly underscored the rights of the people as opposed to chartered corporations in the renowned *Charles River Bridge Case* (1837).

In the meantime the bracing influence of Jacksonian democracy led to the reformation of political practices. The aristocratic caucus system gave way to the open-party convention. The suffrage was further broadened. Presidential electors came to be chosen by the people, and other positions became elective for the first time. Simultaneous to this, and reflecting the same sentiments, a widespread humanitarian movement appeared that aimed at everything from the abolishment of slavery to world peace.

Such, in simplified form, was the dominant (though by no means only) interpretation of Jacksonian America during the first third of this century. The movement toward greater democracy was seen as a powerful, popular force uniting the majority of the people behind their leader, Andrew Jackson. Historians wrote in clear terms of the political movement "Jacksonian Democracy" giving rise to the "Age of the Common Man."

But in the 1920's the Turnerian emphasis on the frontier West as the source of the Jacksonian movement was being modified. Perhaps influenced by the earlier interpretations of Ely and a socialist historian of the Progressive period, Algie M. Simons, Arthur M. Schlesinger, Sr. in a 1922 essay suggested that Jacksonian democracy derived both from the agrarian West and the industrializing Northeast. Specifically Schlesinger claimed that Jackson "could not have

been elected president if the votes of the laboring men of
the Northest had not been added to those of his followers
in the Southeast and West." Like Schlesinger, Charles and
Mary Beard in their monumental *Rise of American Civilization* (1927) emphasized the joint support of farmers and
laborers as the backbone of Jacksonianism. Similarly the
second volume of Vernon Parrington's *Main Currents in
American Thought* (1927), while supporting Turner's emphasis on sectionalism, also stressed the class struggle between workers and capitalists. Schlesinger, the Beards, and
Parrington were all partisan toward Jackson and all saw
the Jacksonian movement as expressing both sectional and
class conflicts.

After 1929 the Depression reinforced the already growing
scholarly interest in the urban-industrial aspects of American history. In that era of class antagonisms and growing
labor power it was only natural that class conflict as a
causal force in history would come to seem even more
significant. This emphasis in interpreting the second quarter of the nineteenth century found its strongest exponent
in Schlesinger's son, Arthur M. Schlesinger, Jr., whose
Pulitzer Prize-winning *The Age of Jackson* appeared in
1945.

While earlier authors had only modified Turner's emphasis on the frontier, Schlesinger rejected it almost entirely. To understand Jacksonian democracy, he contended,
it is best "regarded as a problem not of sections but of
classes." Newly enfranchised eastern laborers, suffering
from deteriorating economic conditions and insecurities
over status, were more sensitive to the economic and social
issues than were other groups. They, therefore, spearheaded
the Jacksonian drive to control the exploitive power of
capitalists groups. Other liberal elements joined them in
the Jacksonian coalition in its historic struggle "to restrain

the power of the business community." This to Schlesinger was the essence not only of Jacksonian democracy but of all American liberalism.

In retrospect, the publication of Schlesinger's *Age of Jackson* distinctly marks a watershed in Jacksonian historiography. On the one hand this work has been the mainspring of modern Jacksonian scholarship, while on the other hand *The Age of Jackson* is the last of a long line of interpretive studies which have seen the Jacksonian era as a period of ideological, economic, and sectional conflict. Viewed in this latter light, Schlesinger's study is a traditional attempt to explain the Jacksonian period within the "progressive" frame of reference; a frame which saw American history as alternating between conservatism and liberalism, the few and the many, the rich and the poor. To Schlesinger "Jacksonian Democracy was . . . a second American phase of that enduring struggle between the business community and the rest of society . . . ."

Since World War II virtually all of Schlesinger's major conclusions have been challenged. Studies by Joseph Dorfman, William A. Sullivan, Richard B. Morris, Edward Pessen, and Walter Hugins have critically examined the thesis that urban workers constituted a major element in the Jacksonian coalition and that labor radicals helped to shape the reform ideology of the Democratic party. Although these historians are by no means in complete accord, several facts do emerge from their varied studies. First, there was nothing like a solid Jacksonian labor bloc. In some areas labor was more Democratic than Whig, while in other localities the reverse was the case. Second, Schlesinger's specific contention that "during the Bank War, laboring men began slowly to turn to Jackson as their leader, and his party as their party," is not born out. In Philadelphia, for example, William Sullivan not only found more workingmen supporting the Whigs than the Democrats, but also that Democratic votes in working-class wards actually declined after the outbreak of the Bank War. In other cities such as Boston and New York, the Democrats gained only slightly among workers in the years of the Bank War. Finally, Jackson's personal sympathy for organized labor was slight. Though he did implement a ten-hour day for federal employees at the Philadelphia naval yard, he also, as Richard Morris has pointed out, was the first president to use federal troops to break up a strike. In a broader sense the aim of the Democratic party "was not," in Joseph Dorfman's words, "to help labor—they generally neglected labor reform—but to create better business conditions."

In place of Schlesinger's urban-labor thesis, Dorfman as well as his Columbia colleague Richard Hofstadter and the bank historian Bray Hammond suggested what has come to be known as the "entrepreneurial" interpretation. Like Schlesinger, they still claimed that economic issues underlay Jacksonian politics; also they continued to view the Jacksonian movement as advancing democracy. But, unlike Schlesinger, they did not see an embattled laboring class and its allies struggling against a capitalist aristocracy. Their Jacksonians as well as their Whigs are essentially middle-class and capitalistic. The conflicts which occur do not pit class against class. Rather they picture a more fraternal and less bitter clash between established Whig entrepreneurs and Jacksonians on-the-make. Jacksonian democracy becomes that of the expectant capitalist who desires only the elimination of special privileges which might check the fulfillment of his aspirations. As Hofstadter wrote of the Jacksonians: "What is demanded is only the classic bourgeois ideal, equality before the law, the restriction of government to equal protection of its citizens. This is the philosophy of a rising middle-class; its aim is not to throttle but to liberate business, to open every possible pathway for the creative enterprise of the people."

More recently, concepts of consensus have been pushed still further. Louis Hartz, Daniel Boorstin, Glyndon G. Van Deusen, Marvin Meyers, and Lee Benson, although willing to admit to some conflicts in Jacksonian America, find fundamental agreement underlying such surface frictions. Americans of both major parties, they contend, operated within a Lockean framework. The goals of capitalism and democracy were accepted by nearly all; party divergences, therefore, were over means, not ends. Meyers even goes so far as to reverse the traditional ideological labels. His Whigs become the liberal party of hope; their program of economic advance "through banks, tariffs, and public promotion of internal improvements" represented "the fulfillment of liberal premises in capitalist progress." The Jacksonians, on the other hand, become the conservative party of fear trying to recapture the Old Republic, "resisting the seductions of risk and novelty, greed and extravagance, rapid motion and complex dealings." Meyers is quick to point out, however, that such differences are of more importance psychologically than economically, and that "both parties . . . reached broadly similar class constituencies."

The natural outcome of the new revisionism expressed by consensus historians has been the rejection of the concept "Jacksonian Democracy." Lee Benson has been the strongest critic of this generalizing label. In *The Concept of Jacksonian Democracy* (1961) Benson correctly shows that this term, though of unknown origin, came into common usage after 1900 and that it became part and parcel of the progressive historians' emphasis on ideological, socioeconomic, and sectional conflict. After careful study of political behavior in New York during the second quarter of the nineteenth century, Benson concludes that none of the underlying assumptions implicit in the term Jacksonian Democracy are valid. "The concept of Jacksonian Democracy," he writes, "has obscured rather than illuminated the course of *New York* history after 1815," and "since events in New York are invariably cited by historians who accept some version of the concept, systematic research may find that in other states the concept also does not conform to reality."

While discarding "Jacksonian Democracy," Benson does not deny that democracy made rapid advances during the period. In fact, like Tocqueville, he associates equality with democracy and claims that during this era an "egalitarian revolution" occurred. "After 1815," he writes, "not only in politics but in all spheres of American life, egalitarianism challenged elitism and, in most spheres and places, egalitarianism won." During these years, according to Benson, America made the "transition from an aristocratic to an egalitarian society." He, therefore, has proposed the substitution of "The Age of Egalitarianism" for the traditional "Age of Jackson."

This consensus school, of which Benson is an articulate representative, has shed a good deal of light on the period from the 1820's through the 1840's, especially in illuminating the unique features of American society compared with Europe. America was more democratic, egalitarian, and nonideological than other nations. Also, in removing the history of this era from the simple dualism of the progressive historians, the subtle complexities of the period become more evident.

However, there are serious limitations to this stress on the values Americans shared in common. For instance, knowing that both Unionists and Confederates during the Civil War believed in constitutional, representative, republican government tells us little about their obvious conflicts. So too for Jacksonian America, the search for consensus beclouds the meaning of the real differences that persons took so seriously. Contemporary beliefs, even if time proves them false, are significant and should be seen as consequential by the historian. For example, it seems evident that many Americans of the 1830's and 1840's felt that aristocracy threatened basic democratic freedoms; they acted and appealed to others on the basis that such beliefs were true. Yet a consensus historian such as Louis Hartz dismisses as "unreal demonology" the persistent label of "aristocracy" that the Jacksonians attempted to pin on the Whigs.

Another major criticism of the consensus historians may be applied to the homogeneous picture they paint of American society. Not only do they see liberal democracy triumphing in the realm of politics, they assume that democracy dominated social and economic life as well. Benson's conception of the age as one of "egalitarianism" implies this. Yet such an interpretation hardly seems warranted in light of the available evidence. As indicated in previous chapters, it was in this period that the generally democratic and agrarian society of farmers, merchants, and craftsmen had begun to give way to a hierarchical, urban-industrial society dominated by an aristocracy of wealth. Instead of increased social and economic equality, the era laid the foundations for the plutocratic and materialistic society of the Gilded Age. In this regard the so-called Age of Jackson might better be described as a way station between the world of Jefferson and that of Grant than as an "Age of Egalitarianism."

It remains, however, to examine in more detail the growth of political democracy in the period. Historians of all schools are in general agreement today that political democracy did not suddenly emerge with the election of Jackson in 1828. In fact, consensus historians such as Robert E. and B. Katherine Brown maintain that well before the Revolution democracy, meaning mainly white manhood suffrage and widespread property holding, was well advanced. Other writers such as Hartz and Boorstin see America as essentially middle-class and democratic throughout its history from colonial settlement to the present. These broad views imply not only that the age of the common man preceded the presidency of Jackson, but that America had always been the land of the common man.

Yet however far back in American history one wishes to push democracy, it is nevertheless true that several specific changes took place preceding Jackson's presidency which make that period appear more democratic politically than any previous era. For one thing, virtually every state by the mid-1820's had extended its franchise to the point where most white males could vote. Some have argued that these suffrage extensions only legalized previous practice. But, however true this might be, another notable change became apparent as the suffrage laws were broadened. The deferential democracy of the Revolutionary period and the first decades of the New Republic in which men of the "better sort" invariably won elections began to give way to a democracy dependent on rhetorical appeals to the common man.

By the 1820's the politician was becoming a specialist— not the statesmen, lawyer, merchant, or planter of an earlier era. Men like Madison, Monroe, and John Quincy Adams—high-minded persons with broad visions— gradually gave way to the professional politicians, the Thurlow Weeds, Amos Kendalls, and Martin Van Burens— individuals who indeed were more concerned with party success than the implementation of principle. Davy Crockett, himself one of the new breed of politicos, once described Van Buren as a man who "could take a piece of meat on one side of his mouth, a piece of bread on the other, and cabbage in the middle, and chew and swallow each in its

severalty, never mixing them together." Crockett's symbolic characterization, allowing of course for the Tennes-
seean's customary exaggeration, could have been applied
to almost any of the political leaders of the time.

Such men depended for their success on highly disci-
plined party organizations that could gain wide popular
support. The concept of party itself was changing in the
decade of the twenties. The traditional view of political
parties, inherited from British and colonial experience, was
a negative one. They were seen as dangerous factions based
on family, friendship, and special interest. The very idea
of a loyal opposition to Washington, Hamilton, and other
early leaders was a contradiction in terms. Opposition to
them bordered on treason. Even Jefferson, the first opposing leader, shared these sentiments. In reflecting on
the final demise of Federalism after the War of 1812, he
wrote: "I fondly hope, 'we may now truly say, we are all
republicans, all federalists,' and that the motto of the
standard to which our country will forever rally, will be,
'federal union, and republican government' . . . ."

Yet in the very "Era of Good Feelings," which Jefferson
had looked forward to as a time when unity and consensus
might prevail, a new attitude of acceptance of party conflict
emerged. During the 1820's in such states as New York,
Pennsylvania, New Jersey, Massachusetts, and North
Carolina, the modern view of parties as necessary democratic devices for shaping and presenting options for popular choice gained widespread acceptance. Instead of personal parties or factions, the advocates of party claimed
that their organizations were democratic associations expressing the will of the majority of the membership.
Loyalty to party, even at the sacrifice of personal principles,
became a positive good. As one party paper expressed it in
1823, "individual partialities and local attachments are
secondary and quite unimportant compared . . . with the

INTERESTS AND PERMANENCY OF THE REPUBLICAN PARTY."

Along with unquestioning support of one's own party, the professional politician of the 1820's showed a growing willingness to accept the existence of an opposition party as a necessary and proper aspect of American politics. Party conflict stirred the people from indifference and stimulated greater party unity. As Van Buren argued in 1827: "In a Government like ours founded upon freedom in thought and action, imposing no unnecessary restraints, and calling into action the highest energies of the mind, occasional differences are not only to be expected, but to be desired. They rouse the sluggish to exertion, give increased energy to the most active intellect, excite a salutary vigilance over our public functionaries, and prevent that apathy which has proved the ruin of Republics." Parties, which gave concrete expression to these "differences," channeled potential violent conflict into verbal and electoral contests between differing democratic institutions. Such parties, according to the New York Governor Enos Throop, "watch and scan each other's doings, the public mind is instructed by ample discussions of public measures, and acts of violence are restrained by the convictions of the people, that the prevailing measures are the results of enlightened reason."

One natural outgrowth of the new type of party organization was the emergence of the convention system as a means of selecting candidates and shaping party positions. Up until the election of 1824, the accepted method of picking candidates had been by a secret caucus of a party's congressional leaders. In that year, however, the caucus proved ineffectual in producing majority agreement within the Republican party; its presidential candidate, William H. Crawford, was a factional choice, and was not able to poll as many votes as the three noncaucus candidates— Jackson, Adams, and Clay. The convention system began

3.   George Caleb Bingham, *Stump Speaking*

to grow on the state and local level from that time, and by the presidential election of 1832 both major parties held national conventions. Conventions satisfied the idea that a party's candidates and positions represented the will of the majority of the members. They also were an effective means of increasing political participation, producing campaign propaganda, and discouraging splits within a party.

Other democratic innovations of the age included the transfer of the election of presidential electors from state legislators to the voters, the increase in the number of elective, rather than appointive, state and local offices, and the replacement of congressmen-at-large with single-member congressional districts. Added to this was the openly avowed notion that state and federal offices belonged to the political victors regardless of training or experience. "No man has any more intrinsic right to official station than another," claimed Jackson in his first Inaugural. "The duties of all public offices are, or at least admit of being made, so plain and simple that men of intelligence may readily qualify themselves for their performance." In less lofty terms Van Buren's friend and fellow member of the Albany Regency, William Marcy, stated matter-of-factly that triumphant politicians "claim as a matter of right the advantages of success. They see nothing wrong in the rule, that to the victor belong the spoils of the enemy."

Undoubtedly all of these changes helped facilitate the rise of the pragmatic, popular, coalition parties which have characterized American political life from Jackson's day to our own, but whether such innovations did indeed make politics more democratic is another matter. Popular concepts of Jacksonian democracy picture a great outpouring of newly enfranchised voters rallying with loud huzzahs around their chosen leaders. Such an image calls to mind the oft reproduced paintings, *Stump Speaking* (plate 3), and *The County Election,* by George Caleb Bingham with their romantic idealization of shirt-sleeved, if slightly besotted, democracy. Or one recalls Tocqueville's surprise at the high level of political participation in America. "The political activity that pervades the United States must be seen in order to be understood," he wrote. "To take a hand in the regulation of society and to discuss it is the biggest concern and, so to speak, the only pleasure an American knows. This feeling pervades the most trifling habits of life; even the women frequently attend public meetings and listen to political harangues . . . ."

However, another astute foreign observer, Harriet Martineau, reached an opposite conclusion. Like many Europeans, Miss Martineau had a preconception of the Ameri-

can as "always talking politics, canvassing, bustling about
to make proselytes abroad, buried in newspapers at home,
and hurrying to vote on election days." But after an inten-
sive two-year investigation of American society, she concluded that apathy, not activity, characterized the ordinary citizen. Recent scholarship supports Martineau's,
not Tocqueville's, evaluation of political participation.
Studies by Richard P. McCormick, Lee Benson, and Robert E. Lane indicate that there was nothing like a great
democratic upsurge in the national elections of the Jacksonian era. As McCormick writes: "The remarkable feature of the vote in the Jackson elections is not its im-
mensity but rather its smallness." In 1828 a little over
fifty-six per cent of adult white males voted; in 1832 at
the height of the Bank War this percentage had declined
to slightly less than fifty-five. On the state and local
level, on the other hand, close contests often saw as
high as eighty per cent participation by eligible voters.
Not until the Log Cabin campaign of 1840, when effective
propaganda and widespread party organization had created a fairly well-balanced two-party system in most
states, did a large proportion of the eligible electorate
turn out to vote for the presidency—about seventy-eight
per cent.

Other supposedly democratizing changes can also be
questioned. Politics of the period had become increasingly
centered around creating a popular image and flattering the
common man. Parades, picnics, and campaigns of personal
slander characterized Jacksonian politicking. But, although
both parties aimed their rhetoric at the people and
mouthed the sacred shibboleths of democracy, this did not
mean that the common man ruled America. The professional politicians coming to the fore in the twenties and
thirties, though sometimes self-made, were seldom ordinary. Both major parties were controled largely by men
of wealth and ambition. Lawyers, newspaper editors, mer-

chants, industrialists, large landholders, and speculators dominated the Democrats as well as the Whigs. Running for high office was becoming increasingly expensive; it has been estimated that campaigning for Congress in 1828 cost about $3,000. Such expenses made it all but impossible for the common man to run unless backed by the party or rich friends.

Similarly, the Jacksonian spoils system failed to put a significant number of lower- or even lower-middle-class persons into appointive positions. In fact a recent study by Sidney H. Aronson on *Status and Kinship in the Higher Civil Service: Standards of Selection in the Administrations of John Adams, Thomas Jefferson, and Andrew Jackson* finds that the type of men appointed to high office in all three administrations were similar in their elitism. "Jefferson and Jackson may have held different ideas about the role of social class in politics than Adams," he concludes, "but they shared with him ideas that stressed the absolute necessity of honesty and efficiency in government. It was for this reason that they were forced to use the same standard utilized by Adams, and by so doing they separated the upper classes from the common people."

In local and state politics, the role of the common man may have been even more nominal than on the national level. Many local office holders received no salaries or ones too small to live on, making these positions generally unattractive except to persons of wealth. Furthermore, on the state or local level it was easier for tight-knit political machines to hold power. Robert Dahl's conclusions in regard to New Haven politics in this period could well be applied to other cities and even states. There, Dahl wrote, "public office was almost exclusively the prerogative of the patrician families," by which he meant those of "wealth, social position and education."

Even the adoption of the convention system on the state and national level did not necessarily assure greater democracy in shaping policy or choosing candidates. In popular thought, the overthrow of "King Caucus" was believed to mark a victory of the people because it removed nominations from the control of a small, secret elite. Yet, as James S. Chase has concluded in a recent article on "Jacksonian Democracy and the Rise of the Nominating Convention," even with the change from caucus to convention, important decisions, including nominations, remained in the hands of an "inner circle of party leaders." Many states had permanent party committees (formal or informal) that controled decisions—the Albany Regency and the Richmond Junto would be the best-known examples of such inner circles. Thus, no matter how representative a convention's delegates were, they were seldom asked to do more than approve of choices made by the party elite.

However, though the common-man rhetoric, spoils system, and nominating conventions may not have actually given the rank-and-file party member an important decision-making role, the psychological belief that politics was becoming more democratic undoubtedly helped to make this so. Popular writing of the time pictured high political office as obtainable by virtually anyone. "The Poorest Boy May Be President," editorialized the St. Louis *Argus* in 1837; the presidency is "within reach of the humblest urchin that roams the streets of our villages . . . . *Liberty and Equality* is the glorious motto of our republic." Furthermore, changes such as the extensions of suffrage represent more than a transformation of the mechanics of voting; they represent a change in republican theory. Earlier republican philosophy saw property holding as essential to political participation. By the twenties, however, this "stake in society" theory had nearly everywhere given way to the idea that at least all white males were entitled to a voice in the running of government. Contempt for the lowly citizen was no longer expressed by the aspiring politician. Instead, frequent flattery and campaign promises to the people by the party politicians helped to stimulate increased political interest and participation, even if not as suddenly and dramatically as once was believed.

Though more persons were taking part in politics, however, neither of the two major parties offered the voters what could truly be called a democratic choice. Both Whigs and Democrats were essentially conservative. Their conservatism was not antidemocratic; opposition to democracy passed from the mainstream of American politics with the unsuccessful stands taken against suffrage extension in the early 1820's by such persons as Justice Joseph Story and Daniel Webster in Massachusetts and Chancellor James Kent in New York. The conservatism of Whigs and Democrats consisted in their cautious attitudes toward new innovations, not in rejecting Lockean liberalism.

Clinton Rossiter, one of the leading historians of conservatism, has listed the five most significant conservative principles in American history as follows: (1) traditionalism—reverential respect for the ideals of the Founding Fathers; (2) unity—belief that loyalty to common values should override particular interests; (3) constitutionalism—belief that the Constitution is a covenant embodying the basic rights of Americans; (4) religion—the belief that divine providence directs the American nation; (5) private property—belief that the right of private property is the most significant American right. With few exceptions, Whigs and Democrats alike shared these conservative values.

Looking at the political issues of the period, this conservatism becomes all the more manifest. In retrospect it is evident that several major issues of overwhelming national importance existed in Jacksonian America. These would include the industrialization and economic growth of the nation with the already apparent tendencies toward concentration and exploitation, slavery, the treatment of minorities and the less fortunate, and the extent and quality of public education. Yet the issues that engaged the two major parties—tariffs and nullification, the Bank War, removal and the Independent Treasury, land laws, internal improvements, Indian policy, Peggy Eaton, and the spoils system—either were not the most significant ones, or where they touched on major problems, they did so in an ineffectual or even negative manner.

The economic growth of the period and the issues related to it are a good example. Because the era of Jacksonian political dominance roughly coincided with the major early revolutions in transportation and industry, it has often been assumed by historians that Jacksonian politics was directly related to these economic changes. This, however, is fallacious. Neither Jacksonian nor Whig politicians had much specific influence on the entrepreneurial innovations of the Boston Associates or other early capitalists, the flow of European capital into America, the massive influx of an immigrant labor force, or the vast expansion of the cotton-plantation economy of the South. The changing tariff policies, according to recent economic historians, seem to have had no measurable correlation with economic growth.

Similarly, Jackson's destruction of the second Bank of the United States was of only minor economic importance. A recent study of *The Jacksonian Economy* by Peter Temin denies that the President's Bank War caused the boom-bust sequence which followed. Yet if this action cannot be blamed for the inflationary spiral that ended disastrously in the depression of 1837, neither can it be credited as a positive cause of economic growth. The major significance of the Bank War was political, not economic.

The liberalization of land laws and the passage of a Preemption Act may have given further motivation to western settlement, though it is unlikely that such legislation greatly increased the numbers of those taking up family farms. Similarly, federal aid to internal improvements, despite Jackson's well-known Maysville Road veto, was of at least minor help in building the nation's transportation system. However, in general, the government under Jackson and Van Buren followed laissez-faire notions and did little to further economic development, while the Whigs, who at least preached a more active neomercantile program of higher protective tariffs, a national bank, and increased aid for internal improvements, never had the opportunity to implement their policies.

When it comes to the more adverse aspects of economic growth—the rising power of the capitalist entrepreneur, the concentration of business into fewer and larger units, the increasing numbers of exploited laborers, and the stratification of society—the national political record of the Jacksonian generation is nearly barren of constructive accomplishments. Despite much rhetorical sympathy for the working class in the campaigns of Whigs and Democrats, little was done to directly aid labor beyond Van Buren's vague 1840 proclamation of a ten-hour day for federal employees on public works. Unquestionably, working conditions were worse at the end of the era than at its outset. Politicians seem to have been unable or unwilling to develop a new democratic ideology relevant to the changing economic realities.

Even less was done by the political leaders to aid the lot of minority groups or the less fortunate. Newer immigrants, as a foreign traveler observed, were "singled out and kept apart, from the mere circumstances of their birth, as a distinct and inferior caste—denounced in the degrading vocabulary of every native American, as unworthy of a more intimate fellowship with him, and in no wise fitted for the enjoyment of that rational freedom and independence, which at another time he claims as of man's inheritance—the inborn right of every human being." Free Negroes, North and South, were discriminated against politically, socially, and economically. So too were white women, especially married women who not only lacked political rights but, in most states, property rights as well. The plight of the insane and seriously sick in Jacksonian society was even more dire. None of these groups were aided by the federal government.

Although the pragmatic politicians of the period tried to avoid the issue of slavery, sensing the divisive effects it would have on the coalition parties, aspects of the slave question could not be excluded entirely from national politics. In judging the dominant Jacksonians on this problem one would have to say that they were proslavery. This is most evident in their attempts to prohibit the circulation of abolitionist materials in the mails. Amos Kendall, as Jackson's Postmaster General, not only allowed southern postal officials to confiscate "inflammatory" mail, he specifically encouraged them. Similarly, it was largely the Democrats who pushed the "gag rule" through the House of Representatives at each session from 1836 to 1844, effectively tabling abolitionist petitions. Other evidence of the proslavery position of the Democrats would include the annexation of slave-holding Texas and the expansion into Mexican territory under the direction of the staunch Jacksonian, President James K. Polk. One might also recall that it was Roger B. Taney, another leading Jacksonian, who as Chief Justice of the Supreme Court wrote the infamous *Dred Scott* decision in 1857.[1] In short, national politics

[1] The *Dred Scott* case in denying black Americans citizenship was not a departure from past precedent, but rather reflected over a generation of federal and state policy. Taney himself, as Jackson's Attorney General in 1831, had written that "the African race in the United States even when free are everywhere a degraded class, and exercise no political influence . . . . [They] are permitted to be citizens by the sufferance of the white population and hold whatever rights they enjoy at their mercy."

throughout the era was dominated by proslavery sentiment.

More actively antidemocratic than the proslavery policies followed by the Jacksonians was their Indian policy.
Andrew Jackson's Indian program was a simple one, consisting of driving the remaining eastern tribes to the west
of the Mississippi. He pursued this plan with a vigor and
ruthlessness that showed more zeal than even his battle
against Biddle's Bank. Overriding treaties, the Supreme
Court, and human decency, Jackson succeeded in pushing
such civilized tribes as the Cherokees, Choctaws, and
Chickasaws from their lands to the unfamiliar and hostile
western prairies. This policy not only violated Indian rights,
it also indirectly aided the further spread of slavery since
the appropriated Indian lands were nearly all in the South.

The failure of the two major parties to confront basic
issues, or to do so in a less than democratic manner, helps
explain the extensive organized activity outside of major
party channels during the second quarter of the nineteenth
century. There were widespread demands for social and
economic change; but, since established political institutions discouraged innovation, persons seeking change felt
forced to create new institutions. The existence of ideological third parties such as the Working Men's parties or the
Liberty party, an active trade union movement, numerous
reform societies, and a variety of utopian communities all
indicate a frustration with traditional institutions. So too
does the appearance and growth of new millennial religious
sects such as the Mormons and the Millerites.

On a cruder level the anxieties and frustrations of the
period often vented themselves in acts of violence. Like
today, the Jacksonian era was marked by riots, street fights,
and incendiarism. From formal duels, to less aristocratic
wrestling and gouging matches, to organized lynchings and
gang fights, violence was endemic to America. But more

surprising than the extent of such brutal behavior was the fact that much of it was aimed at achieving social, economic, and political change. Examples of this are many, including such well-known instances as the Nat Turner uprising, the Black Hawk and Second Seminole wars, the successful Anti-Rent Wars along New York's Hudson Valley, and Rhode Island's Dorr Rebellion.

In the nation's burgeoning cities riots often revealed sharp class, ethnic, and racial antagonisms. The rich and respectable expressed fears of open class warfare. Philip Hone confessed in his diary after New York City's catastrophic 1835 fire that he was "alarmed by some of the signs of the times which this calamity has brought forth: the miserable wretches who prowled about the ruins, and became beastly drunk on the champagne and other wines and liquors with which the streets and wharves were lined, seemed to exult in the misfortune, and such expressions were heard as 'Ah! they'll make no more five per cent dividends!' and 'This will make the aristocracy haul in their horns!' " A few years later during the depression of the late thirties, a New York magazine writer observed growing signs of unrest. From everywhere "comes rumor after rumor of riot, insurrection, and tumult." In 1841 another New Yorker expressed fear of the "noisy and tumultuous masses—shouting for change, reform, and progress."

During these years mob violence was a not uncommon feature of New York life. There were the Park Theatre riots in 1831 and 1836, the Irish-American election riots of 1834 and 1838, the "stonecutters" riot and the abolitionist riots of 1834, the bread riots of 1837, the anti-German riots of 1840, and riots among the Irish laborers working on the Croton aqueduct that same year. In 1842 there were election riots, in 1843 angry workingmen attacked the tracks and property of the Harlem Railroad. Perhaps the most clear-cut example of violence motivated by class hatred occurred at the end of the period in the Astor Place Opera House riot of 1849. Philadelphia, Baltimore, and Boston witnessed similar periodic outbreaks of organized violence often directed against bankers and so-called "monopolists."

Michel Chevalier, reflecting on the violence in America of the 1830's, found such disruptions all too frequent. In a chapter entitled "Symptoms of Revolution," he noted that "unfortunately, reverence for the laws seems to be disappearing among Americans." The United States, in his view, had come to be characterized by "scenes of murder, outrage, and destruction . . . both in the slaveholding States and in those in which slavery does not exist, in the country as well as in the towns, at Boston, the republican city *par excellence,* as well as at Baltimore, . . . good citizens have repeated with grief: 'We are in the midst of a revolution.'" What was particularly alarming to Chevalier about these disorders was not just "their general prevalence and frequent repetition," but even more the fact that "their importance is little realized. They meet with few voices to condemn them, but they find many to excuse them."

Chevalier saw the crisis as a failure of the political order to keep pace with the rapid process of economic and social change. "The present generation in the United States," he wrote, "brought up in devotion to business, living in an atmosphere of self-interest, if it is superior to the last generation in commercial intelligence and industrial enterprise, is inferior to it in civil courage and love of the public good." The American political system, Chevalier concluded, "no longer works well . . . . Everywhere, the relations established by the old federal compact are unfitted to the new state of things."

Assuming the basic validity of Chevalier's analysis, several important conclusions concerning this period of

American history become apparent. First, though the interpretation that consensus historians have given seems reasonably accurate as a description of major party *politics* (the Whigs and Democrats being by-and-large nonidiological, pragmatic coalitions, made up of politicians whose primary objective was electoral success).[2] The broader implications of the consensus historians that the major parties mirrored the homogeneous, compromising nature of American society as a whole does not hold up. Conflict was as characteristic of the age of consensus. Social cohesion was maintained, but at the expense of individuals and minorities. Organized ideological protest and out-and-out violence were common occurrences.

Second, the concentration on major party politics gives a misleading picture of the period. Washington was physically and psychologically distant from the ordinary American. The issues that dominated national politics, although of some importance and generating some excitement, were not the most relevant. Furthermore, the tendency of historians to dwell upon political, public rhetoric has obscured the greater impact of social and economic change. The emergence of both a new moneyed aristocracy and a propertyless proletariat, for example, may have been overlooked in the past because of their low visibility within the political context.

Third, this was not the era of "Jacksonian Democracy," nor even the "Age of Jackson." Certainly Andrew Jackson was a significant political figure whose strong personality stamped itself on the period's politics. Yet the advancement of democracy in many instances preceded the ascendency of Jackson to the presidency, while on other occasions the

[2] This is not to say that all conflicts or ideological differences between Whigs and Democrats were ficticious. Recent studies by Frank Otto Gatell, Robert V. Remini, and Donald B. Cole, for instance, indicate that the Whig party appealed more to the upper economic classes than did the Democrats.

party of Jackson obstructed rather than furthered democratic causes. As has been shown, on many basic issues the Jacksonians were conservative or downright antidemocratic. But even more questionable than the concept "Jacksonian Democracy" applied to the politics of the period, is the use of the label the "Age of Jackson" to describe the era as a whole. The most significant economic, social, and intellectual developments of the time had almost nothing to do with Jackson or his party's policies. Contemporary foreign analysts of American society were aware of this. None of them used the name of Jackson in their book titles; nor did they see him as the dominant figure in American life. The two most penetrating studies— Tocqueville's and Chevalier's—give Jackson scant attention. Even the ardent Jacksonian, Francis Grund, mentions Jackson on only four pages of his 783-page study of *The Americans in Their Moral, Social, and Political Relations* (1837). Subsequent historians, however, predisposed toward political history, almost invariably made use of the convenient, though misleading, "presidential synthesis." Such a synthesis inevitably leads to an oversimplified view of American history, and this is especially true of the pre-Civil War period when the federal government was limited in functions both because of its physical isolation and the dominant laissez-faire ideology.

Fourth, the concept "Age of Egalitarianism" which has been advanced as a replacement for "Jacksonian Democracy" must also be rejected. Except on the level of political and popular rhetoric, the period from the mid-1820's to the late 1840's was no more democratic than preceding or following decades. While existing wages and future opportunities were somewhat greater for workers and farmers here than for their European counterparts, the percentage of those climbing the mythic American success ladder from rags-to-riches was small. The United States was a class-structured society, and, rather than disappearing, class lines were tightening. By the 1840's American society was unquestionably more socially stratified than in the 1820's.

Finally, then, this was neither an era of egalitarian, complacent consensus, nor simply one of polarized class or sectional conflict. Perhaps a phrase vague enough to encompass the complexities of the period, while at the same time explicit enough to have conceptual merit, would be "The Age of Innovation." It appeared to contemporaries as a time of rapid change, and repeated historical investigations have validated this judgment. Innovations affected almost all aspects of American society in the generation after the War of 1812, and by the end of the 1830's it was evident that life would no longer be so simple, self-sufficient, rural, agrarian, decentralized, Anglo-Saxon, and Protestant. Both buoyant optimism and anxious uncertainties were generated as the country became more industrial, urban, centralized and stratified, but less homogeneous and communal. Rationalism was giving way to romanticism, self-sufficiency to capitalism, craftsmanship to mass production, sail to steam, European involvement to isolationist expansionism, deferential politics to demagogic democracy, traditional society to modern America. It was, in short, an Age of Innovation.

SELECTED BIBLIOGRAPHY

IN THE FOLLOWING ALPHABETICAL LISTING OF PRIMARY AND secondary literature bearing on the period from 1820 to 1850, I have not attempted to be inclusive; a truly comprehensive bibliography would fill several volumes. My selection has been guided by two criteria. First, I have listed those works discussed or quoted in the text. Second, I have included writings which have influenced my interpretation.

More extensive bibliographies on the Middle Period can be found in Arthur M. Schlesinger, Jr., *The Age of Jackson,* Boston, 1945, pp. 529–559; Glyndon G. Van Deusen, *The Jacksonian Era, 1828–1848,* New York, 1959, pp. 267–283; and Edward Pessen, *Jacksonian America: Society, Personality, and Politics,* Homewood, Ill., 1969, pp. 352–393. Useful historiographical discussions of Jacksonian literature include Alfred A. Cave, *Jacksonian Democracy and the Historians,* Gainesville, Fla., 1964; Charles Grier Sellers, Jr., "Andrew Jackson Versus the Historians," *Mississippi Valley Historical Review,* XLIV (March 1958), 615–634; William G. Morgan, "John Quincy Adams Versus Andrew Jackson: Their Biographers and the 'Corrupt Bargain' Charge," *Tennessee Historical Quarterly,* XXVI (Spring 1967), 43–58; John William Ward, "The Age of the Common Man," in John Higham, ed., *The Reconstruction of American History,* New York, 1962, pp. 82–97.

Adams, Henry. *The Education of Henry Adams.* New York, 1942.
———. *The United States in 1800.* Ithaca, 1955.
Adams, John and Jefferson, Thomas. *The Adams-Jefferson Letters.* Ed. Lester J. Cappon. 2 vols. Chapel Hill, 1959.
Adams, John Quincy. *Diary of John Quincy Adams.* New York, 1929.
Adams, William Forbes. *Ireland and Irish Emigration to the New World From 1815 to the Famine.* New Haven, 1932.
Albion, Robert Greenhalgh. *The Rise of New York Port, 1815–1860.* New York, 1939.
American Whig Review. New York, 1845–52.
Amory, Cleveland. *The Proper Bostonians.* New York, 1947.
Appleton, Nathan. *Introduction of the Power Loom and Origin of Lowell.* Lowell, 1858.

Aristocracy of Boston. Boston, 1848.

Arky, Louis. "The Mechanics' Union of Trade Associations," *Pennsylvania Magazine of History and Biography,* LXXVI (April 1952), 142–176.

Armstrong, William. *The Aristocracy of New York: Who They Are, and What They Were; Being a Social and Business History of the City for Many Years.* New York, 1848.

Aronson, Sidney H. *Status and Kinship in the Higher Civil Service: Standards of Selection in the Administrations of John Adams, Thomas Jefferson, and Andrew Jackson.* Cambridge, Mass., 1964.

Asbury, Herbert. *The Gangs of New York.* New York, 1937.

Baltzell, E. Digby. *Philadelphia Gentlemen: The Making of a National Upper Class.* Glencoe, Ill., 1958.

Bancroft, George. *History of the United States.* 10 vols. Boston, 1834–74.

————. *Literary and Historical Miscellanies.* New York, 1855.

Bassett, John Spencer. *The Life of Andrew Jackson.* 2 vols. Garden City, N. Y., 1911.

Batchelder, Samuel. *Introduction and Early Progress of the Cotton Manufacture in the United States.* Boston, 1863.

Bathe, Greville and Dorothy. *Oliver Evans.* Philadelphia, 1935.

Beach, Moses Yale. *Wealth and Biography of the Wealthy Citizens of New York City . . . .* 6th ed. New York, 1845.

Beard, Charles and Mary. *The Rise of American Civilization.* 2 vols. New York, 1927.

Beecher, Lyman. *Autobiography.* Ed. Barbara M. Cross. 2 vols. Cambridge, Mass., 1961.

————. *A Plea for the West.* Cincinnati, 1835.

Benson, Lee. *The Concept of Jacksonian Democracy: New York as a Test Case.* Princeton, 1961.

————. "Research Problems in American Political Historiography," in *Common Frontiers of the Social Sciences,* ed. Mirra Komarovsky. Glencoe, Ill., 1957.

Berthoff, Rowland T. "The American Social Order: A Conservative Hypothesis," *American Historical Review,* LXV (April 1960), 495–514.

————. *British Immigrants in Industrial America.* Cambridge, Mass., 1953.

Bestor, Arthur E. *Backwoods Utopias.* Philadelphia, 1950.

Bigelow, Jacob. *Elements of Technology.* 2nd ed. Boston, 1831.

Billington, Ray Allen. *The Protestant Crusade, 1800–1860.* Chicago, 1964.

[Boardman, James]. *America, and the Americans.* London, 1833.

Bode, Carl. *The Anatomy of American Popular Culture, 1840–1861*. Berkeley and Los Angeles, 1959.

Bodo, John R. *The Protestant Clergy and Public Issues, 1812–1848*. Princeton, 1954.

Bolles, Albert S. *Industrial History of the United States*. Norwich, Conn., 1879.

Boorstin, Daniel J. *The Americans: The National Experience*. New York, 1967.

Bowers, Claude G. *The Party Battles of the Jackson Period*. Boston, 1922.

Bowron, Bernard, Marx, Leo, and Rose, Arnold. "Literature and Covert Culture," *American Quarterly,* IX (Winter 1957), 377–386.

Bremner, Robert H. *From the Depths: The Discovery of Poverty in the United States*. New York, 1956.

Bridges, William E. "Family Patterns and Social Values in America, 1825–1875," *American Quarterly,* XVII (Spring 1965), 3–11.

Bristed, Charles Astor. *The Upper Ten Thousand: Sketches of American Society*. New York, 1852.

Brooks, Van Wyck. *The World of Washington Irving*. New York, 1944.

Brown, Richard H. "The Missouri Crisis, Slavery and the Politics of Jacksonianism," *South Atlantic Quarterly,* LXV (Winter 1966), 55–72.

Brown, Robert E. *Middle-Class Democracy and the Revolution in Massachusetts, 1691–1780*. Ithaca, 1955.

Brown, Robert E. and B. Katherine. *Virginia, 1705–1786: Democracy or Aristocracy?* East Lansing, Mich., 1964.

Brownson, Orestes A. "The Labouring Classes," *The Boston Quarterly Review* (July 1840).

Bruchey, Stuart. *The Roots of American Economic Growth, 1607–1861*. New York, 1968.

Buckingham, James Silk. *America, Historical Statistical, and Descriptive*. 3 vols. London, 1841.

Burt, Nathaniel. *The Perennial Philadelphians: The Anatomy of an American Aristocracy*. Boston, 1963.

Bushnell, Horace. *Christian Nuture*. New York, 1876.

Byllesby, Langdon. *Observations on the Sources and Effects of Unequal Wealth*. New York, 1826.

Cady, Edwin Harrison. *The Gentleman in America: A Literary Study in American Culture*. Syracuse, 1949.

Calhoun, Arthur W. *A Social history of the American Family*. 3 vols. Cleveland, 1917–19.

Calhoun, Daniel H. *Professional Lives in America: Structure and Aspiration, 1750–1850.* Cambridge, Mass., 1965.

Carey, Henry C. *Miscellaneous Works.* Philadelphia, 1865.

———. *Principles of Political Economy.* Philadelphia, 1837.

Carey, Mathew. *Appeal to the Wealthy of the Land . . . .* Philadelphia, 1833.

———. *Essays on Political Economy.* Philadelphia, 1822.

———. *Miscellaneous Pamphlets.* Philadelphia, 1831.

Cave, Alfred A. *Jacksonian Democracy and the Historians.* Gainesville, Fla., 1964.

Chase, James Staton. "Jacksonian Democracy and the Rise of the Nominating Convention," *Mid-America,* XLV (October 1963), 229–249.

Chesterfield, Lord. *The American Chesterfield.* Philadelphia, 1833.

Chevalier, Michel. *Society, Manners, and Politics in the United States: Letters on North America.* Ed. John William Ward. Garden City, N.Y., 1961.

Cheyney, Edward P. *The Anti-Rent Agitation in the State of New York, 1839–1846.* Philadelphia, 1887.

Christman, Henry. *Tin Horns and Calico . . . .* New York, 1961.

Clark, Victor S. *History of Manufactures in the United States, 1607–1860.* 3 vols. Washington, D.C., 1916.

Cobbett, William. *The Emigrant's Guide.* London, 1830.

Cochran, Thomas C. "Did the Civil War Retard Industrialization?" *Mississippi Valley Historical Review,* XLVIII (September 1961), 197–210.

———. "The Social Sciences and the Problem of Historical Synthesis," *The Social Sciences in Historical Study,* Social Science Research Council, Bulletin 64 (1954), 157–171.

———, and Miller, William. *The Age of Enterprise . . . .* New York, 1942.

Cole, Charles C. *The Social Ideas of the Northern Evangelists, 1826–1860.* New York, 1954.

Cole, Donald B. "The Presidential Election of 1832 in New Hampshire," *Historical New Hampshire,* XXI (Winter 1966), 32–50.

Collins, S. H. *The Emigrant's Guide to the United States of America.* London, 1830.

Colton, Calvin. *The Americans.* London, 1833.

———. *Manual for Emigrants to America.* London, 1832.

———. *Public Economy for the United States.* New York, 1848.

Commons, John R. and associates, eds. *A Documentary History of American Industrial Society.* 10 vols. Cleveland, 1910–11.

_____. *History of Labour in the United States.* 4 vols. New York, 1918–35.

Coolidge, John. *Mill and Mansion: A Study of Architecture and Society in Lowell, Massachusetts, 1820–1865.* New York, 1942.

Cooper, James Fenimore. *The American Democrat.* New York, 1956.

_____. *Home as Found.* New York, 1896.

_____. *Notions of the Americans Picked Up by a Travelling Bachelor.* 2 vols. New York, 1963.

Coxe, Tench. *A View of the United States* . . . . Philadelphia, 1794.

Crockett, Davy. *An Account of Col. Crockett's Tour to the North and Down East.* Philadelphia, 1835.

Cross, Whitney R. *The Burned-over District: The Social and Intellectual History of Enthusiastic Religion in Western New York, 1800–1850.* New York, 1965.

Cunliffe, Marcus. *The Nation Takes Shape: 1789–1837.* Chicago, 1959.

Curtis, George W. *The Potiphar Papers.* New York, 1854.

Dahl, Curtis. "The American School of Catastrophe," *American Quarterly,* XI (Fall 1959), 380–390.

Dahl, Robert A. *Who Governs? Democracy and Power in an American City.* New Haven, 1961.

Daniels, George H. *American Science in the Age of Jackson.* New York, 1967.

David, Paul A. "The Growth of Real Product in the United States before 1840," *Journal of Economic History,* XXVII (June 1967), 151–195.

Davis, David Brion. *Homicide in American Fiction, 1798–1860: A Study in Social Values.* Ithaca, 1957.

_____. "Some Themes of Counter-Subversion: An Analysis of Anti-Masonic, Anti-Catholic, and Anti-Mormon Literature," *Mississippi Valley Historical Review,* XLVII (September 1960), 205–224.

Dayton, Abram C. *Last Days of Knickerbocker Life in New York.* New York, 1897.

Democratic Review. New York, 1837–50.

Dickens, Charles. *American Notes for General Circulation.* New York, 1942.

Dorfman, Joseph. *The Economic Mind in American Civilization.* 3 vols. New York, 1946–49.

_____. "The Jackson Wage-Earner Thesis," *American Historical Review,* LIV (January 1949), 296–306.

Drescher, Seymour. *Dilemmas of Democracy: Tocqueville and Modernization.* Pittsburgh, 1968.

[Dwight, Theodore]. *The Northern Traveller*. New York, 1826.

Eaton, Clement. *The Growth of Southern Civilization*. New York, 1961.

Elkins, Stanley, and McKitrick, Eric. "A Meaning for Turner's Frontier," *Political Science Quarterly*, LXIX (September and December 1954), 321–353, 565–602.

Elkins, Stanley. *Slavery, A Problem in American Institutional and Intellectual Life*. Chicago, 1959.

Ely, Richard T. *The Labor Movement in America*. New York, 1886.

Emerson, Ralph Waldo. *The Complete Essays and Other Writings of Ralph Waldo Emerson*. New York, 1940.

Ernst, Robert. *Immigrant Life in New York City, 1825–1863*. New York, 1949.

Evans, Oliver. *The Young Mill-Wright & Miller's Guide*. 4th ed. Philadelphia, 1821.

Everett, Edward. *Orations and Speeches on Various Occasions*. 4 vols. Boston, 1878–79.

Finney, Charles Grandison. *Charles Grandison Finney's Autobiography*. New York, 1876.

————. *Lectures on Revivals of Religion*. Ed. William G. McLoughlin. Cambridge, Mass., 1960.

Fish, Carl Russell. *The Rise of the Common Man, 1830–1850*. New York, 1927.

Fisher, Marvin. *Workshops in the Wilderness: The European Response to American Industrialization, 1830–1860*. New York, 1967.

Fishlow, Albert. *American Railroads and the Transformation of the Ante-Bellum Economy*. Cambridge, Mass., 1965.

Flexner, James Thomas. *That Wilder Image: The Painting of America's Native School from Thomas Cole to Winslow Homer*. Boston, 1962.

Flint, Timothy. *Recollections of the Last Ten Years*. Ed. C. Hartley Grattan. New York, 1932.

Fogel, Robert William. *Railroads and American Economic Growth* . . . . Baltimore, 1964.

Foster, Sir Augustus John. *Jeffersonian America: Notes on the United States of America Collected in the Years 1805-6-7 and 11-12* . . . . Ed. Richard Beale Davis. San Marino, Calif., 1954.

Foster, Charles I. *An Errand of Mercy: The Evangelical United Front, 1790–1837*. Chapel Hill, 1960.

Frelinghuysen, Theodore. *An Inquiry into the Moral and Religious Character of the American Government*. New York, 1838.

Gallman, Robert E. "Commodity Output, 1839–1899," in *Trends in the American Economy in the Nineteenth Century*, ed. William N. Parker. Princeton, 1960.

Gatell, Frank Otto. "Money and Party in Jacksonian America: A Quantitative Look at New York City's Men of Quality," *Political Science Quarterly,* LXXXII (June 1967), 235–252.

Gates, Paul W. *The Farmer's Age: Agriculture 1815–1860.* New York, 1962.

Genovese, Eugene D. "Marxian Interpretations of the Slave South," in *Towards a New Past,* ed. Barton J. Bernstein. New York, 1968.

_____. *The Political Economy of Slavery.* New York, 1965.

Gitelman, H. M. "The Waltham System and the Coming of the Irish," *Labor History,* VIII (Fall 1967), 227–253.

Godey's Lady's Book. Philadelphia, 1830–50.

Goodman, Paul. "Ethics and Enterprise: The Values of a Boston Elite, 1800–1860," *American Quarterly,* XVIII (Fall 1966), 437–451.

Graham, Hugh Davis and Gurr, Ted Robert, eds. *The History of Violence in America: Historical and Comparative Perspectives.* New York, 1969.

Grantham, Dewey W., Jr. *The Democratic South.* New York, 1965.

Greeley, Horace. *Recollections of a Busy Life.* New York, 1868.

Green, Fletcher M. "Democracy in the Old South," *Journal of Southern History,* XII (February 1946), 3–23.

Griffin, Clifford S. *Their Brothers' Keepers: Moral Stewardship in the United States, 1800–1865.* New Brunswick, N. J., 1960.

Grimsted, David. *Melodrama Unveiled: American Theater and Culture, 1800–1850.* Chicago, 1968.

Griscom, John H. *The Sanitary Condition of the Laboring Population of New York.* New York, 1845.

Grund, Francis J. *The Americans in their Moral, Social, and Political Relations.* Intro. Douglas T. Miller. 2 vols. New York, 1969.

_____. *Aristocracy in America . . . .* Intro. George E. Probst. New York, 1959.

Gusfield, Joseph R. *Symbolic Crusade: Status Politics and the American Temperance Movement.* Urbana, Ill., 1963.

Guttmann, Allen. *The Conservative Tradition in America.* New York, 1967.

Habakkuk, H. J. *American and British Technology in the Nineteenth Century.* Cambridge, Eng., 1962.

Hall, Captain Basil. *Travels in North America in the Years 1827 and 1828.* 3 vols. Edinburgh, 1829.

Hall, James. *Letters From the West.* Intro. John T. Flanagan. Gainesville, Fla., 1967.

Hamilton, Thomas. *Men and Manners in America.* 2 vols. Edinburgh, 1833.

Hammond, Bray. *Banks and Politics in America from the Revolution to the Civil War.* Princeton, 1957.

———. "Jackson, Biddle and the Bank of the United States," *Journal of Economic History,* VII (May 1947), 1–23.

Handlin, Oscar. *Boston's Immigrants.* Cambridge, Mass., 1941.

Hansen, Marcus Lee. *The Atlantic Migration, 1607–1860.* New York, 1961.

Harris, Neil. *The Artist in American Society: The Formative Years, 1790–1860.* New York, 1966.

Harris, Seymour E., ed. *American Economic History.* New York, 1961.

Hartz, Louis. *The Liberal Tradition in America.* New York, 1955.

Hawthorne, Nathaniel. *The Complete Novels and Selected Tales of Nathaniel Hawthorne.* New York, 1937.

———. *Passages from the American Note-Books.* Boston, 1883.

[Hazard, T. R.] *Facts for the Laboring Man.* Newport, 1840.

Henig, Gerald S. "The Jacksonian Attitude toward Abolitionism in the 1830's," *Tennessee Historical Quarterly,* XXVIII (Spring 1969), 42–56.

Hofstadter, Richard. *The American Political Tradition.* New York, 1948.

Hone, Philip. *The Diary of Philip Hone, 1828–1851.* Ed. Allan Nevins. New York, 1936.

Hugins, Walter. *Jacksonian Democracy and the Working Class: A Study of the New York Workingmen's Movement 1829–1837.* Stanford, 1960.

Hunt's Merchant's Magazine and Commercial Review. New York, 1839–50.

Irving, Washington. *The Sketch Book.* New York, 1954.

Jaher, Frederic C., ed. *The Age of Industrialism in America.* New York, 1968.

Jerome, Harry. *Migration and the Business Cycles.* New York, 1926.

Jones, Peter d'A. *America's Wealth: The Economic History of an Open Society.* New York, 1963.

Josephson, Hannah. *The Golden Threads: New England's Mill Girls and Magnates.* New York, 1949.

Kendall, Amos. *Autobiography of Amos Kendall.* New York, 1949.

[Kennedy, J.] *Defense of the Whigs.* New York, 1844.

Kent, William, ed. *Memoirs and Letters of James Kent, LL.D.* Boston, 1898.

Kerr, John. *Rip Van Winkle.* Philadelphia, 1829.

Kirkland, Mrs. C. M. *The Evening Book.* New York, 1851.

Kouwenhoven, John A. *Made in America: The Arts in Modern Civilization.* Garden City, N. Y., 1949.

Krout, John Allen and Fox, Dixon Ryan. *The Completion of Independence, 1790–1830.* New York, 1944.

Kuznets, Simon. "National Income Estimates for the United States Prior to 1870," *Journal of Economic History,* XII (Spring 1952), 115–130.

Lane, Robert E. *Political Life.* Glencoe, Ill., 1959.

Lane, Roger. *Policing the City: Boston 1822–1885.* Cambridge, Mass., 1967.

Larcum, Lucy. *A New England Girlhood.* New York, 1961.

Larkin, Oliver. *Art and Life in America.* New York, 1949.

Latrobe, John H. B. *The First Steamboat Voyage on the Western Waters.* Baltimore, 1871.

Lawrence, Amos. *Extracts from the Diary and Correspondence of the Late Amos Lawrence.* Boston, 1855.

The Laws of Etiquette. Philadelphia, 1836.

Layer, Robert G. "Wages, Earnings, and Output in Four Cotton Textile Companies in New England, 1825–1860," Ph.D. dissertation, Harvard University, 1952.

Lebergott, Stanley. "Wage Trends, 1800–1900," in *Trends in the American Economy in the Nineteenth Century,* ed. William N. Parker. Princeton, 1960.

Lebowitz, Michael A. "The Jacksonians: Paradox Lost?" in *Towards a New Past,* ed. Barton J. Bernstein. New York, 1968.

Lewis, R. W. B. *The American Adam.* Chicago, 1955.

Lipset, Seymour Martin. *Political Man: The Social Bases of Politics.* New York, 1963.

———, and Bendix, Reinhard. *Social Mobility in Industrial Society.* Berkeley and Los Angeles, 1959.

Litwack, Leon F. *North of Slavery: The Negro in the Free States, 1790–1860.* Chicago, 1961.

Livermore, Shaw, Jr. *The Twilight of Federalism: The Disintegration of the Federalist Party, 1815–1830.* Princeton, 1962.

Lodge, Henry Cabot. *Early Memories.* New York, 1913.

Loveland, Ann C. "Evangelicalism and 'Immediate Emancipation' in American Antislavery Thought," *Journal of Southern History,* XXXII (May 1966), 172–188.

The Lowell Offering. Lowell, 1840–45.

Luther, Seth. *Address to the Working Men of New England.* Boston, 1832.

Lyell, Sir Charles. *Travels in North America.* 2 vols. New York, 1845.

McClelland, Peter D. "Railroads, American Growth, and the New Economic History: A Critique," *Journal of Economic History,* XXVIII (March 1968), 102–123.

McCormick, Richard P. "New Perspectives on Jacksonian Politics," *American Historical Review,* LXV (January 1960), 288–301.

―――. *The Second American Party System . . . .* Chapel Hill, 1966.

―――. "Suffrage, Classes and Party Alignments: A Study of Voter Behavior," *Mississippi Valley Historical Review,* XLVI (December 1959), 397–410.

MacDonald, William. *Jacksonian Democracy, 1829–1837.* New York, 1906.

McFaul, John Michael. "The Politics of Jacksonian Finance," Ph.D. dissertation, University of California, Berkeley, 1963.

McGouldrick, Paul F. *New England Textiles in the Nineteenth Century.* Cambridge, Mass., 1968.

McKinley, Blaine E. "The Stranger in the Gates: Employer Reactions Toward Domestic Servants in America 1825–1875," Ph.D. dissertation, Michigan State University, 1969.

McLoughlin, William G. *Modern Revivalism.* New York, 1959.

McMaster, John Bach. *The Acquisition of Political, Social, and Industrial Rights in America.* New York, 1961.

―――. *A History of the People of the United States, From the Revolution the Civil War.* 8 vols. New York, 1883–1913.

Mahon, John K. *History of the Second Seminole War, 1835–1842.* Gainesville, Fla., 1967.

Mailloux, Kenneth F. "The Boston Manufacturing Company of Waltham, Massachusetts, 1813–1848: The First Modern Factory in America," Ph.D. dissertation, Boston University, 1957.

Main, Jackson Turner. *The Social Structure of Revolutionary America.* Princeton, 1965.

Mann, Horace. *Life and Works of Horace Mann.* Ed. M. T. P. Mann. 3 vols. Boston, 1865–68.

Mannheim, Karl. *Essays on the Sociology of Culture.* London, 1956.

Marryat, Captain Frederick. *A Diary in America.* London, 1839.

Marshall, Lynn L. "The Strange Stillbirth of the Whig Party," *American Historical Review,* LXXII (January 1967), 445–468.

Martineau, Harriet. *Society in America.* Ed. and intro. Seymour Martin Lipset. Gloucester, Mass., 1968.

Marx, Leo. *The Machine in the Garden.* New York, 1967.

Meir, Hugo A. "Technology and Democracy, 1800–1860," *Mississippi Valley Historical Review,* XLIII (March 1957), 618–640.

Melville, Herman, *Mardi and a Voyage Thither.* New York, 1964.

_____. *Selected Tales and Poems.* Ed. Richard Chase. New York, 1956.

Meyers, Marvin. *The Jacksonian Persuasion: Politics and Belief.* New York, 1960.

Milbank, Jeremiah, Jr. *The First Century of Flight in America.* Princeton, 1943.

Miles, Henry A. *Lowell as it Was and as it Is.* Lowell, 1845.

Miller, Douglas T. "Immigration and Social Stratification in Pre-Civil War New York," *New York History,* XLIX (April 1968), 156–168.

_____. *Jacksonian Aristocracy: Class and Democracy in New York, 1830–1860.* New York, 1967.

Miller, Lillian B. "Painting, Sculpture and the National Character, 1815–1860," *Journal of American History,* LIII (March 1967), 696–707.

_____. *Patrons and Patriotism: The Encouragement of the Fine Arts in the United States, 1790–1860.* Chicago, 1966.

Miller, Perry. *The Life of the Mind in America.* New York, 1965.

_____. *Nature's Nation.* Cambridge, Mass., 1967.

Mirsky, Jeannette and Nevins, Allan. *The World of Eli Whitney.* New York, 1952.

Montgomery, David. "The Working Classes of the Pre-Industrial American City, 1780–1830," *Labor History,* IX (Winter 1968), 3–22.

Moore, Barrington, Jr. *Social Origins of Dictatorship and Democracy.* Boston, 1966.

Morris, Richard B. "Andrew Jackson, Strikebreaker," *American Historical Review,* LV (October 1949), 54–68.

Mowatt, Anna Cora. *Fashion; or, Life in New York.* New York, 1849.

Murray, Charles Augustus. *Travels in North America During the Years 1834, 1835, and 1836.* 2 vols. New York, 1839.

New York Herald. 1835–50.

New York Tribune. 1841–50.

Nichols, Roy F. *The Invention of Political Parties.* New York, 1967.

Nichols, Thomas Low. *Forty Years of American Life, 1821–1861.* New York, 1937.

Niles' Weekly Register. Baltimore, 1811–49.

North, Douglass C. "Early National Income Estimates of the U.S." *Economic Development and Cultural Change,* IX (April 1961), 387–396.

_____. *The Economic Growth of the United States, 1790–1860.* New York, 1966.

North American Review. Boston, 1815–50.

Norton, A. B. *The Great Revolution of 1840: Reminiscences of the Log Cabin and Hard Cider Campaign.* Mount Vernon, Ohio, 1888.

Noyes, John Humphrey. *A History of American Socialisms.* New York, 1870.

Nye, Russel Blaine. *The Cultural Life of the New Nation, 1776-1830.* New York, 1960.

———. *George Bancroft.* New York, 1964.

Ostrander, Gilman. *The Rights of Man in America, 1606-1861.* Columbia, Mo., 1960.

Owsley, Frank. *Plain Folk of the Old South.* Baton Rouge, 1949.

Parrington, Vernon L. *Main Currents in American Thought.* 3 vols. New York, 1927-30.

Parton, James. *The Presidency of Andrew Jackson.* Ed. Robert V. Remini. New York, 1967.

Paulding, James Kirke. *The Diverting History of John Bull and Brother Jonathan.* New York, 1835.

Persons, Stow. "The Cyclical Theory of History in Eighteenth Century America," *American Quarterly,* VI (Summer 1954), 147-163.

Pessen, Edward. *Jacksonian America: Society, Personality, and Politics.* Homewood, Ill., 1969.

———. *Most Uncommon Jacksonians: The Radical Leaders of the Early Labor Movement.* Albany, 1967.

———. "The Working Men's Party Revisited," *Labor History,* IV (Fall 1963), 203-226.

Peterson, Merrill D. *The Jefferson Image in the American Mind.* New York, 1962.

Potter, David M. *People of Plenty: Economic Abundance and the American Character.* Chicago, 1954.

Raymond, Daniel. *Thoughts on Political Economy.* Baltimore, 1820.

Remini, Robert V. *Andrew Jackson.* New York, 1966.

———. *Andrew Jackson and the Bank War.* New York, 1967.

———. *Martin Van Buren and the Making of the Democratic Party.* New York, 1959.

Rezneck, Samuel. "The Rise and Early Development of Industrial Consciousness in the United States, 1760-1830," *Journal of Economic and Business History,* IV (August 1932), 784-811.

Riegel, Robert. *Young America, 1830-1840.* Norman, Okla., 1949.

Rossiter, Clinton L. *Conservatism in America.* New York, 1955.

Rostow, Walt W. *The Stages of Economic Growth.* Cambridge, Eng., 1960.

Rowe, Kenneth Wyer. *Mathew Carey: A Study in American Economic Development.* Baltimore, 1933.

Sanford, Charles L. *The Quest for Paradise: Europe and the American Moral Imagination.* Urbana, Ill., 1961.

Schlesinger, Arthur M. *Learning How to Behave: A Historical Study of American Etiquette Books.* New York, 1946.

_____. *New Viewpoints in American History.* New York, 1922.

Schlesinger, Arthur M., Jr. *The Age of Jackson.* Boston, 1945.

_____. *Orestes A. Brownson: A Pilgrim's Progress.* Boston, 1939.

Schlissel, Lillian. "John Quidor in New York," *American Quarterly,* XVII (Winter 1965), 756–760.

Schouler, James. *History of the United States of America Under the Constitution.* 6 vols. New York, 1894–1904.

[Scoville, Joseph A.] *The Old Merchants of New York.* 5 vols. New York, 1863–66.

Seaman, Ezra C. *Essays on the Progress of Nations, in Civilization, Productive Industry, Wealth and Population.* New York, 1853.

Sellers, Charles Grier, Jr. "Andrew Jackson Versus the Historians," *Mississippi Valley Historical Review,* XLIV (March 1958), 615–634.

Shlakman, Vera. "Economic History of a Factory Town: A Study of Chicopee, Massachusetts," *Smith College Studies in History,* XX (October 1934, January, April, July, 1935), Nos. 1–4.

Silby, Joel H. *The Shrine of Party: Congressional Voting Behavior, 1841–1852.* Pittsburgh, 1967.

Simons, Algie M. *Social Forces in American History.* New York, 1911.

Simpson, Stephen. *The Working Man's Manual: A New Theory of Political Economy, on the Principle of Production the Source of Wealth.* Philadelphia, 1831.

Skidmore, Thomas. *The Rights of Man to Property!* . . . New York, 1829.

[Smith, Benjamin, ed.] *Twenty-Four Letters From Labourers in America to Their Friends in England.* London, 1829.

Smith, Henry Nash. *Virgin Land: The American West as Symbol and Myth.* New York, 1959.

Smith, Margaret E. *The First Forty Years of Washington Society.* Ed. Gaillard Hunt. New York, 1906.

Smith, Timothy L. "Protestant Schooling and American Nationality, 1800–1850," *Journal of American History,* LIII (March 1967), 679–695.

_____. *Revivalism and Social Reform.* New York, 1957.

Somkin, Fred. *Unquiet Eagle: Memory and Desire in the Idea of American Freedom, 1815–1860.* Ithaca, 1967.

Stone, Richard Gabriel. *Hezekiah Niles as an Economist.* Baltimore, 1933.

Strassmann, W. Paul. *Risk and Technological Innovation: American Manufacturing Methods During the Nineteenth Century.* Ithaca, 1959.

Strong, George Templeton. *The Diary of George Templeton Strong, 1835–1875.* Eds. Allan Nevins and Milton Halsey Thomas. 3 vols. New York, 1953.

Stuart, James. *Three Years in North America.* 2 vols. Edinburgh, 1833.

Sullivan, William A. "Did Labor Support Andrew Jackson?" *Political Science Quarterly,* LXII (December 1947), 569–580.

———. *The Industrial Worker in Pennsylvania, 1800–1840.* Harrisburg, Pa., 1955.

Sumner, William Graham. *Andrew Jackson as a Public Man.* Boston, 1882.

Sydnor, Charles S. *The Development of Southern Sectionalism, 1819–1848.* Baton Rouge, 1948.

———. "The One-Party Period of American History," *American Historical Review,* LI (April 1946), 439–451.

Taylor, George R. "American Economic Growth Before 1840: An Exploratory Essay," *Journal of Economic History,* XXIV (December 1964), 427–444.

———. "American Urban Growth Preceding the Railway Age," *Journal of Economic History,* XXVII (September 1967), 309–319. \

———. *The Transportation Revolution, 1815–1860.* New York, 1951.

Taylor, William R. *Cavalier and Yankee.* New York, 1963.

Temin, Peter. *The Jacksonian Economy.* New York, 1969.

———. "Steam and Water Power in the Early Nineteenth Century," *Journal of Economic History,* XXVI (June 1966), 187–205.

Thomas, Brinley. *Migration and Economic Growth: A Study of Great Britain and the Atlantic Economy.* Cambridge, Eng., 1954.

Thomas, John L. "Romantic Reform in America, 1815–1865," *American Quarterly,* XVII (Winter 1965), 656–681.

Thomas, Nathan G. "The Second Coming in the Third New England: The Millennial Impulse in Michigan, 1830–1860." Ph.D. dissertation, Michigan State University, 1967.

Thoreau, Henry David. *Walden and Other Writings of Henry David Thoreau.* New York, 1937.

de Tocqueville, Alexis. *Democracy in America.* Ed. Phillips Bradley. 2 vols. New York, 1945.

———. *Journey to America.* Ed. J. P. Mayer. New Haven, 1960.

Trollope, Frances. *Domestic Manners of the Americans.* Ed. Donald Smalley. New York, 1960.

Tryon, Rolla M. *Household Manufactures in the United States, 1640–1860.* Chicago, 1917.

Tucker, George. *The History of the United States from their Colonization to the End of the Twenty-Sixth Congress in 1841.* 4 vols. Philadelphia, 1856–57.

_____. *Progress of the United States in Population and Wealth in Fifty Years.* New York, 1964.

Tuckerman, Henry T. *America and Her Commentators.* New York, 1961.

Turner, Frederick Jackson. *The Frontier in American History.* New York, 1962.

_____. *The United States, 1830–1850.* New York, 1965.

Tuveson, Ernest Lee. *Millennium and Utopia.* New York, 1964.

_____. *Redeemer Nation: The Idea of America's Millennial Role.* Chicago, 1968.

Tyler, Alice Felt. *Freedom's Ferment.* Minneapolis, 1944.

Van Buren, Martin. *The Autobiography of Martin Van Buren.* Ed. John C. Fitzpatrick. American Historical Association, *Annual Report.* Washington, 1920.

Van Deusen, Glyndon G. *The Jacksonian Era, 1828–1848.* New York, 1959.

_____. "Some Aspects of Whig Thought and Theory in the Jacksonian Period," *American Historical Review,* LXIII (January 1958), 305–322.

Voice of Industry. Lowell and Boston, 1845–48.

Von Holst, Herman E. *The Constitutional and Political History of the United States.* 8 vols. Chicago, 1876–1892.

von Nardroff, Ellen. "The American Frontier as a Safety Valve—The Life, Death, Reincarnation, and Justification of a Theory," *Agricultural History,* XXXVI (July 1962), 123–142.

Wade, Richard C. *The Urban Frontier.* Chicago, 1964.

Waldo, Samuel Putnam. *Memoirs of Andrew Jackson.* Hartford, 1819.

Wallace, Michael. "Changing Concepts of Party in the United States: New York 1815–1828," *American Historical Review,* LXXIV (December 1968), 453–491.

Ward, John William. *Andrew Jackson: Symbol for an Age.* New York, 1962.

Ware, Caroline. *The Early New England Cotton Manufacture.* Boston, 1931.

Ware, Norman. *The Industrial Worker, 1840–1860.* Boston, 1924.

Webster, Daniel. *Writings and Speeches of Daniel Webster.* 18 vols. Boston, 1903.

Wecter, Dixon. *The Saga of American Society: A Record of Social Aspirations, 1607–1937.* New York, 1937.

Weed, Thurlow. *Autobiography of Thurlow Weed.* Boston, 1883.

Welter, Barbara. "The Cult of True Womanhood, 1820–1860," *American Quarterly,* XVIII (Summer 1966), 151–174.

Welter, Rush. "The Frontier West as Image of American Society: Conservative Attitudes before the Civil War," *Mississippi Valley Historical Review,* XLVI (March 1960), 593–614.

White, George S. *Memoir of Samuel Slater, The Father of American Manufactures. Connected with a History of the Rise and Progress of the Cotton Manufacture in England and America.* Philadelphia, 1836.

Whitehouse, Arch. *The Early Birds: The Wonders and Heroics of the First Decades of Flight.* Garden City, New York, 1965.

Wilburn, Jean Alexander. *Biddle's Bank.* New York, 1967.

Willard, Emma. *An Address to . . . the Legislature of New York Proposing a Plan for Improving Female Education.* Albany, 1819.

Williams, William Appleman. "The Age of Mercantilism: An Interpretation of the American Political Economy, 1763 to 1828," *William and Mary Quarterly,* XV (October 1958), 419–437.

Williamson, Chilton. *American Suffrage: From Property to Democracy, 1760–1860.* Princeton, 1960.

Wilson, Major L. "Andrew Jackson: The Great Compromiser," *Tennessee Historical Quarterly,* XXVI (Spring 1967), 64–78.

———. "The Concept of Time and the Political Dialogue in the United States, 1828–48," *American Quarterly,* XIX (Winter 1967), 619–644.

Wise, Gene. "Political 'Reality' in Recent American Scholarship: Progressives versus Symbolists," *American Quarterly,* XIX (Summer 1967), 303–328.

Wishy, Bernard. *The Child and the Republic: The Dawn of Modern American Child Nuture.* Philadelphia, 1968.

Working Man's Advocate. New York, 1830–36.

Wyllie, Irvin G. *The Self-Made Man in America.* New York, 1966.

Young, Mary E. "Indian Removal and Land Allotment: The Civilized Tribes and Jacksonian Justice," *American Historical Review,* LXIV (October 1958), 31–45.

Zetterbaum, Marvin. *Tocqueville and the Problem of Democracy.* Stanford, 1966.

INDEX